FASTNET

One Man's Voyage

The Roger Vaughan Library

DAVID
Ninety-Four and Counting - A Pudding full of Plums

THE MEDAL MAKER
Biography of Victor Kovalenko

CLOSING THE GAP
World Sailing's Emerging Nations Program

THE STRENUOUS LIFE OF HARRY ANDERSON

SAILING ON THE EDGE
(contributor)

DROPPING THE GLOVES
Inside the Fiercely Competitive World of Professional Ice Hockey

GOLF: THE WOMAN'S GAME

MUSTIQUE II

LISTEN TO THE MUSIC
The Life of Hilary Koprowski

TONY GWYNN'S THE ART OF HITTING

NASCAR: THE INSIDE TRACK

MUSTIQUE

AMERICA'S CUP XXVII
The Official Record

HERBERT von KARAJAN

FASTNET: ONE MAN'S VOYAGE

TED TURNER: THE MAN BEHIND THE MOUTH

THE GRAND GESTURE

RHODE ISLAND: A SCENIC DISCOVERY

FASTNET

One Man's Voyage

By Roger Vaughan

1979 Author's Reissue 2019
Choptank Word Bank

The Roger Vaughan Library

Originally published in 1980 by Seaview Books

Reissued in 2019 by Choptank Word Bank
Bachelor's Point, Oxford, Maryland
www.choptankwordbank.com

ISBN: 978-1-7333135-0-6
Library of Congress Control Number: 2019909874

Cover and Interior Design: Joseph Daniel

POD Edition
Printed in the United States

Welcome to my reissue of FASTNET: ONE MAN'S VOYAGE, about the 1979 Fastnet Race originally published in 1980. It is reissued on the 40th anniversary of that most famous Fastnet Race during which a vicious storm crippled the fleet of over 300 boats. Fifteen sailors perished.

I was on board the maxi, Kialoa, fulfilling an assignment to write about the boat's owner, Jim Kilroy. The perilous nature of the event – what evolved as a journey to the edge of disaster – caused my report to become a more comprehensive picture of how people in such a dire situation react, and what they contemplate.

Not a word has been changed from the original book. I thought about rewriting parts of it, making a few changes, adding a few updates, possibly cutting a few inflammatory bits, but I ended up being convinced it is important to maintain the book as a period piece that reflects the politics, the culture, and the state of affairs at the time it was written.

Roger Vaughan
Oxford, Maryland
2019

This book is for F. Ivan, my father
Stephen, my brother

FASTNET

Kialoa *sailing close-hauled in 20 knots of wind.*

ONE

John B. (Jim) Kilroy, owner of Kialoa.

Circumstance, not choice, places one in the middle of such a maelstrom. While the encounter is not one a sane person openly wishes for, going to sea implies taking the risk. Therefore, when it happens, there can be no recriminations, no regrets. One must respond the best one can to the test, and enjoy the rare opportunity – the privilege in fact – that brings vessel, gear, and crew close to an outer limit of strength, resourcefulness, and endurance. We didn't beat the storm on *Kialoa*. But it didn't beat us either. And that is the best one can do.

Fingers writing about
the Fastnet Race
The New York Times
September 2, 1979

How typical that passage is of Fingers, reeking as it does of toughness, don't look back, veins in your teeth, and sea chanties if not Marine Corps hymns. It reveals one of his more stoic sets of mind, nurtured forever by his parents telling him long ago about the sea captain in his lineage. New England heartiness. And perhaps by his recent fascination with Clint Eastwood movies, their nonstop brutal action occasionally interrupted by a few menacing words spoken quietly through clenched teeth. Those in whom he had confided his mad notion to rebuild his image after Eastwood had smiled and assured him that fortunately he would never pull it off. Fingers readily entertained notions. Even though few of them stuck for very long, his ability to consider so many possibilities dismayed him even as it pleased him. He was glad to have the space open for new concepts, but it worried him that at forty-two he had quite so much space available. One was supposed to be more settled at forty-two, more defined.

A friend of Fingers' sought him out after the above piece was published to admonish him. I was with you, the friend told him, right up to that stuff about recriminations and regrets. What do you mean, taking away my recriminations and regrets! Every time I go sailing I have regrets. After about two hours I want to be home getting warm and watching TV and having a lot of Cokes. This brought Fingers off his horse because the friend was an old friend and a dear one who very well might have known him better than he knew himself. Only a fool postures before such a friend. It would be pointless to deny that during the interminable night in the middle of the storm-lashed Irish Sea, with the air temperature at fifty-five degrees, and seventy-five-knot gusts heaving water around and producing a wind-chill factor of god-knows-what that sliced through his foul-weather gear and sadistically pressed his soaked inner garments against his skin, he had suffered a few recriminations himself. But, he had assured his friend, he hadn't deserved them.

On *Kialoa*, we began to feel the storm at 6 p.m. (Greenwich Mean Time) Monday evening, August 13. We were sailing in St. George's Channel, the southernmost portion of the Irish Sea that lies between Land's End on the southwest tip of England and southern Ireland. At noon that day, in gray weather and a light breeze, we had been the first boat around Fastnet Rock, a lighthouse on a rock off the Irish coast that is the first mark of the course. The race had been an uneventful light-air contest to that point. The sea had been smooth. With her tall rig easily driving her slim, seventy-nine-foot canoe hull, *Kialoa* had been making marvelous time. *Condor*, a seventy-seven-footer that had shown us the best competition over the first leg of the race, was more than an hour behind us at the Rock. With more than half the six-hundred-five-mile course behind us, things were looking good for *Kialoa*.

Owner Jim Kilroy was being cautiously optimistic. Kilroy has made millions as an industrial-real-estate developer in Los Angeles. Next to doing that, he loves racing on the ocean. Unlike many of the men who own the bigger race boats, Kilroy is very much the captain of his yacht. He is a good helmsman, tactician, and navigator. He is a devotedly analytical man who lives by his Hewlett-Packard 67 calculator as Jesse James lived by his gun. He had a session with the H-P at the Rock, then casually mentioned that we were about an hour ahead of the Fastnet course record (seventy-nine hours, two minutes) set by Ted Turner on *American Eagle* in 1971. Men who own the biggest boats are always thinking about records. Kilroy said we had a chance to break the record, if the wind held up. *If* the wind held up.

At the time Kilroy's speculation was innocent enough. We had received reports of a storm center building in the Atlantic, a hundred miles or so to the west of us, but it wasn't expected to send us more than edge effects. And it didn't. But recalling Jim's concern about the wind holding up did provide a welcome chuckle later that night.

By 9 p.m. sleep was out of the question for those of us off watch, such were the steep angles of roll to either side, and the shuddering blows felt throughout the boat as the bow smashed into seas. For *Kialoa* to be tossed about in such a manner something big had to be brewing. The barometer was down and dropping. Kilroy climbed out of his bunk and called all hands on deck. You can sleep any time, this tall, lean man of fifty-seven said as he pulled a stocking cap over hair that has been snow white since his mid-thirties: this is what we came for.

While we had been below, the other watch had gone through the gamut of sail changes as the wind increased, from the number-one jib (the largest) and full mainsail to the number-four jib and triple-reefed main. The anemometer was pegged at sixty knots, and the gusts were hitting us in staggering combinations. The seas were very large, and building.

We moved about the deck in a crouch, hanging on with care while moving the clip of our safety harnesses from one point to another. A change to the number-five jib had been called for. We raised a small staysail (a sail that rigs like a jib halfway between the bow and the mast) to keep the boat in balance between jibs, and took the number four down with difficulty. An hour later we would have had to cut it loose. Other boats, we learned later, had indeed resorted to the knife. Other crews cut the sheet and watched heavy headsails flail themselves to shreds in a matter of minutes.

As it was, the spray coming off the bow struck us like whips. Only our safety lines clipped to the weather side kept us from sliding into the sea. Raising the number five was out of the question. The wind was increasing. We would sail with the small staysail and the main reefed to maximum.

As Fingers came on deck he was handed a safety harness that had been carefully folded and made fast with elastic bands. The neatly stowed packet was typical of *Kialoa* organization. He slipped the bands and noticed it was a Lirakis harness. Steve Lirakis, a twelve-meter sailor and long-time windsurfer from Newport, Rhode Island, was an acquaintance. He knew Lirakis had put a lot of work into the harnesses, a lot of testing. The nylon webbing felt strong and new. Twist it, pull at it, the stitching wouldn't budge. The safety line itself was six feet long, giving the wearer a twelve-foot working circle, and the snap hook at its end was stainless steel and stiffly sprung. Good goods. In the light from the hatch Fingers noticed the belt was blue and red. It occurred to him how sharp it would look against the white foul-weather jacket he had borrowed from the boat's gear. He chided himself good-naturedly for this blatant bit of vanity and smiled inwardly at the exchange. He pulled the belt snug against his chest. It felt good. He was ready.

Fingers's reaction to the storm was restrained enthusiasm. One must forgive him this apparently callous, perhaps even foolhardy feeling, because this was a working trip, and he was prepared to take it as it came, as usual. A storm meant action, and action meant a chance to observe this three-quarter-million-dollar vessel, its highly touted crew, and its formidable owner-skipper with their collective backs against the wall. It would be a rare opportunity. The fact that he was also a part of the crew was so much the better. A long-time sailor, he could handle it, and it afforded him a catbird seat.

He liked to write about people who hung it out, and the best way to write about such people, he found, was to hang it out with them and get the feel.

Over the past fifteen years he had been launched from and landed on a carrier, flown in hot-air balloons, made a parachute jump, climbed the towers of New York's Verrazano Bridge when it was under construction, been wrung out in an open cockpit stunt plane, trekked through the Himalayas for two weeks, toured Europe with Bob Dylan, been on a crusade in Hawaii with Billy Graham, been plucked off the deck of a destroyer by sling lowered from a helicopter, picked strawberries and bunked with migrant workers in Salinas, California, and more. He was a determined participant.

Fingers had always considered these ventures the very best part of a line of work that he loved. The life suited his inquisitive nature—his habitually red-lined metabolic rate that had earned him the nickname Fingers—his experiential lust.

Yet he was anything but a daredevil. Risking life and limb for the hell of it was unsettling to him. Couching it in work—the need to know—was something else. Work was the key word. The rationale, springing as it did from the good old Protestant ethic (a painful admission), fit. When it was work, something took him over. It was like a photographer he knew who couldn't handle the sight of blood, but who had been able to photograph major surgical operations when the day rate was right.

He believed in his work, he tried to live by its rules (don't anticipate!), and he had decided long ago something that Jimmy Carter should have known: he would always eat the beans. That came from one of several Theoretical Dilemmas that used to be traded around an office where he once worked, as a measure of one's mental mettle. On assignment in Mexico an impoverished family invites you to dinner. They serve a very spicy dish containing mostly beans with a few other, mysterious ingredients thrown in. If you eat the meal you will be sick. To refuse it would be a terrible insult. What do you do? Fingers never thought there was any real question about that, and had had a number of opportunities to put the beans where his mouth was.

His life did tend to make him a touch flaky. While others in his line of work brought home strange souvenirs to hang on their walls, Fingers carried back weird fragments of people, conversations, and cultural extracts that would rattle around in his head for months, creating disturbance therein. When *the* subject of the early 1960s was drugs, naturally Fingers had to find out what that was all about. In the interest of good reporting, of course. His need to fool around with drugs had been constant since then. It was nothing serious, mind you, just some weed, actually a little more than some, more than that, actually, if the truth were known, and maybe a little yellow painkiller once in a while to steady down the old fast-lane metabolism so he could take stock of things, and on the rare occasion a little toot of coke, only when someone came around with it—he never kept any in his own drawer, or only very rarely, because he didn't like it that much (it always made his heart pound) and the price was out of his reach, frankly.

None of this could be held against Fingers because his record was good. He was responsible. He produced. He was on time. He was ready for whatever. And he kept a low profile (don't interfere with the flow of events), like now, as he came on watch and pulled the safety harness snug around his chest and took in the wild night, the steep seas, the bodies huddled together on the weather rail, the boat thrashing through the maelstrom at twelve knots, heaving and jolting like a runaway stagecoach. Going to his knees for balance, he crawled up the slanting deck to a place on the rail, clipped his lifeline to a stanchion base, and put his back into the blow like a steer in a blizzard. But, inside, his heart had skipped a beat. He would have preferred to hoot and holler at least once.

In pursuit of their destiny, storms evolve, build, meander a path of least resistance, and move on or blow out. It caused one to wonder how it was that a storm of this magnitude, with its unusually nasty disposition, had pulled itself together to strike the Fastnet fleet of three hundred three vessels with full ferocity, perfect timing, and faultless aim. Members of a more primitive society than ours would have quaked at the gods' obvious wrath and taken immediate steps toward appeasement. Sacrificial virgins at least. Because this was not just another storm.

Storms of various magnitudes are occurring all the time around the globe. Some of the most vicious happen in remote or unoccupied areas, and are of interest only to meteorologists. To gain notoriety, a storm must cause measurable destruction. The storm that would hit the Fastnet fleet on Monday evening, August 13, had been born four days earlier over the Great Lakes in the United States. It was a weak storm carrying tropical air that began its delinquency by dropping tornadoes over the Ohio valley as it traveled an easterly course.

On August 10, the storm had proceeded into the Gulf of Maine, and was causing thunderstorms in Massachusetts and Connecticut. A few storm-related fatalities were recorded. The storm also created excitement for sailors competing in the J-24 World Championships in Newport, Rhode Island. Thirty-five knot winds struck the eighty-boat fleet, capsizing several boats and breaking gear.

The storm system, still a small, weak low-pressure disturbance, continued moving eastward at about forty knots. At noon (GMT) on Sunday, August 12, it was located four hundred miles east-southeast of St. John's, Newfoundland. According to Robert Rice, chief meteorologist for Weather Services Corporation in Boston, at that point the storm was going through an area of light support. The positions of long wave ridges (high-pressure areas) and long wave troughs (lows) tend to be relatively predictable in the Northern Hemisphere. That is, they can be located in the same general areas with regularity. The long wave ridge to the southeast of St. John's was doing little to enhance the storm. The storm was moving but not developing. It had a vertical depth of about five thousand feet on Sunday the twelfth, a far cry from major storm depth of fifty thousand to sixty thousand feet.

By noon (GMT) on Monday, August 13, the storm had crossed the Atlantic and was positioned five hundred miles southwest of Fastnet Rock. It was registering a pressure of one thousand seven millibars then (one thousand millibars equals thirty inches of mercury, or normal atmospheric pressure). "A pimple," Rice calls it at that point. But now it was entering the periphery of the Icelandic Low, sliding off an upper-level high-pressure ridge into a trough. It hit the jackpot in the form of a pool of very cold air aloft that was in a perfect position to move in. The air pool carried temperatures of minus twenty-five to thirty degrees Celsius, unusual for that time of year. That is the kind of super cold air that nourishes the vicious winter storms that regularly lash the Irish Sea.

The storm system eagerly sucked the cold air in through its wake, and in just six hours it had acquired considerable muscle. By 6 p.m. (GMT) its center was within one hundred fifty miles of the southwestern tip of Ireland, and it now measured nine hundred ninety-five millibars. It was deepening rapidly, Rice says.

Storms will usually attain wind speeds relative to their pressure gradient. A given millibar spacing will support a certain amount of wind. But if the pressure of a storm system falls rapidly, more air will force its way in and the resulting wind speeds will be higher than what might be expected—so-called super-gradient winds. The Fastnet storm was a rapidly developing system. Rice would give it a score of eight out of ten so far as speed of development was concerned. In just two hours, from 7 p.m. to 9 p.m. (GMT), the pressure dropped from nine hundred ninety-five to nine hundred eighty-nine millibars. "Three millibars per hour," Rice says, "is a very big drop. Impressive." Somewhere near midnight on Monday the storm peaked, with a millibar reading of nine hundred seventy-five to nine hundred eighty. The storm had attained maximum development in just twelve hours. Rice says that is extraordinary.

The explosive growth of the storm was the key to its violent nature. The rapid change of pressure produced gusting in excess of seventy knots. Since it was a young storm, it didn't cover much territory. It remained small, forcing the high winds within it to race around in a tight, cyclonic (counterclockwise) pattern. As such a storm passes over an area, the wind shifts will be more pronounced, more frequent. For those at sea, the Fastnet storm came out of the south, veered to the south-south-west, and ended up blowing out of the northwest. Winds of fifty to more than seventy knots rotated one hundred twenty degrees in twelve hours!

Major disruption of the sea resulted. Not only were the waves stirred up by the high winds large ones, but they were approaching from several directions at once. The line of waves from the south had no time to dissipate before the southwest lines began, and they were still coming when the lines from the northwest were blown up. There was a high frequency of rogue waves. Add to that condition the funnel-like topography of the Irish Sea, and the way the ocean bottom shoals to one hundred feet or less as one moves south from Fastnet Rock, and one begins to understand just how perilous the situation was, especially for those boats that were still trying to beat into the wind and seas in order to round Fastnet Rock. As yacht racing chronicler Jack Knights wrote in Sports Illustrated, "Yachtsmen began to relearn that in gusts of more than 60 knots craft under 40 feet cannot make progress against the wind. Those under 30 feet become fully occupied with the simple necessity of staying afloat." Before the long night ended, fifteen sailors would be dead.

The thirty- to forty-foot waves were closely spaced. Four hundred feet—measured from crest to crest— was the best estimate of Bruce Kendall, *Kialoa*'s sailing master. Kendall is a brawny, taciturn New Zealander who has been with Kilroy as skipper and watch captain for eleven years. In that time he has sailed two hundred thousand miles over the world's oceans. Kendall is a complete sailor. He can build boats, sail them, race them, and keep all systems running.

Kendall said that a typical South Seas storm might have larger waves, but they would be spaced normally at fifteen hundred feet, making them less steep. The seas of the Fastnet storm were very steep. Sailors call such seas "square," perhaps because that is how they feel when a boat is trying to combat them—like too many miles of bad road.

Members of the daily press who wrote about the Fastnet storm described boats falling off the sides of these waves, implying that boats actually went airborne, landing kerplunk in the troughs. That was certainly an exaggeration on the part of landlocked writers who were doing their best to deliver the full dramatic treatment they thought the subject deserved. And it was, after all, a period of otherwise slow news.

But those writers were on the right track. What happened was this: As yachts that were moving along broadside to these waves were drawn up their sides, they would begin to lose buoyancy on the down (lee) side. This would increase their angle of heel. The higher they rose on the side of the wave, the steeper it would become and the more they would heel. Further, the wind speed was about twenty knots higher on the top of the wave than on the bottom. So here a yacht would be, already heeling at a hellish angle, getting slammed by an extra twenty knots of wind when she needed it least. If the wave happened to be breaking on top, she would get rocked by tons of water in addition. Smacko. It was such a situation that knocked two *Kialoa* crewmen off the rail toward the middle of the boat where they fetched up on their lifelines with a jerk, and then bounced back to land on Jim Kilroy's back. Kilroy had seen the cresting sea coming and braced himself on a winch. The two careening bodies crushed him against it, ribs first. He went grudgingly below in pain with two broken ribs and a protruding piece of dislocated cartilage that would be his permanent souvenir of the race.

The conditions put the mast tips of several fifty-footers in the water. Many forty-footers put their mast tips in the water for long counts while everything from anchors to frying pans and people were uprooted and flung about down below. And vessels under forty feet caught the most hell. Some of them rolled over completely, three hundred sixty degrees: mast tip in the water, mast tip pointing at the bottom, mast and rigging carried away as gravity reclaimed the keel, then popping right side up with lines and rigging and other gear looking like the aftermath of an explosion in a pasta factory. Olive oil on the overhead. And with people badly hurt, or gone, or maybe just half-drowned, scared to death.

It was a storm with a disposition frightening enough to cause strange behavior within the fleet. Like the sudden confidence exhibited in life rafts. There are good life rafts (not many), but even a good raft is only as reliable as its record of maintenance and safety in-spection is long. On most boats the life raft is a joke. It shouldn't be, and maybe life-raft technology will improve to the point that it won't be, but at the pres-ent time the life raft is a cumbersome, heavy, required piece of gear with a reputation only slightly above that of the town drunk. Life rafts aren't often spoken about without being preceded by a disparaging modifier, as in "the fucking (insert brand name)."

And yet many crews on yachts that were having a rough time went immediately to the life rafts. Even assuming that all the rafts launched were the best that money could buy and in perfect condition, this reaction remains a puzzlement. The first thing any kid learns before going boating is to stay with the boat if anything happens. Stay with the boat. Rule number one. It is posted on the camp bulletin board. Later on, one perhaps runs into Shakespeare's *The Tempest*, in which the same point is implicit. During that storm, the various noblemen on board scream their last words of despair into the gale and plunge into the sea. Prospero, whose magic caused the storm, asks the spirit Ariel, "Who was so firm, so constant, that this [turmoil] would not infect his reason?" And Ariel answers, "Not a soul but felt a fever of the mad, and play'd some tricks of desperation. All but mariners plung'd in the foaming brine and quit the vessel."

All but mariners. Shakespeare's vessel, with its mariners safely tucked below, survives the storm and makes it to a nearby port. Of the three hundred three yachts in the Fastnet Race, only five went to the bottom. Those who have analyzed the grim tally agree that taking prematurely to life rafts was a major cause of death in the Fastnet Race. The reason is clear: A raft was no match for that storm, even if it could have been successfully launched and boarded. Seven of the fifteen deaths were raft-related.

Aboard *Aries*, one of the hot U.S. Admiral's Cup boats, the life raft was floated out of its compartment behind the helmsman by a torrent of water that came aboard during one knockdown. A crewman grabbed for it as it went past, clutched at a line hanging from it, held on, felt it give, and realized he had pulled the ripcord. There, on the deck of *Aries*, a forty-six-footer in full, semicontrolled flight, a ten-man raft began to inflate. A push-pull ensued. The deck crew wanted it shoved below. The folks below said no thanks. *Aries* crashed on through the night. The helmsman began having trouble seeing past the expanding rubber bag. Two crewmen pulled knives and began stabbing it to death, a task complicated by the raft's many compartments. When the raft had finally been subdued, someone asked if he should take it below and patch it in case they needed it later on. That was good for a laugh, and during such a night laughs were at a premium.

It wasn't Fingers' first storm. When he was eighteen he had shipped aboard a leaky wooden forty-footer that shouldn't have been taken more than twenty miles offshore. He had helped race it to Bermuda. Call it youthful enthusiasm.

The owner, a newcomer to the sport who was finally dissuaded from stuffing the bilges with live lobsters, had selected a crew of unseamanlike friends and a rusty navigator. Halfway to Bermuda this aging vessel and her complement of weekend sailors ran out of luck and encountered a hurricane.

In the middle of the dirty gray night that followed, when Fingers was at the helm running before the blow under bare masts at nine knots watching huge seas trying to come aboard (some did), he had a passing consideration that this was it. In his compulsion to use the bilges for something, the owner had stowed canned goods there with their labels still attached. The great quantity of water-soaked paper that resulted did a proper job of clogging the bilge pumps. Up forward, water poured down into the vessel through two anchor-line ports that hadn't been plugged. For a while the old boat was in danger of sinking.

Everyone aboard was soaked, bruised, and exhausted. But between attacks of vomiting the landlubbers kept bailing. When the storm abated, the navigator, whose major accomplishment had been to keep the vessel in the storm longer than any boat in the fleet, managed to locate Bermuda and aim for it once again.

Fingers' second memorable storm had hit him deep in the Himalayas in the form of a marvelously crazed twenty-year-old Yale coed who caused what appeared to be extreme palpitations of the heart. The turmoil was later diagnosed as "approaching forty," but not before parts of the rig had been carried away and substantial damage had been done to permanent dockage arrangements halfway around the world. That one wasn't just another storm, either.

And now this. Fingers sat on the rail being pelted by wind-driven water and bounced against the hard aluminum deck as *Kialoa* pitched and rolled. It took both hands to hold on. He knew that to make it through this night with any degree of success he had first to attain a proper attitude. He selected a few chips from the stack and worked on plugging them into his central nervous system. Patience. Humor. Alertness. Relaxation. Endurance.

Attitude was critical to performance and hence survival, he knew that. There were two schools of thought. One longtime ocean sailor he knew approached bad weather with hostility. The man had once admitted that at the helm during storms he found himself giving the finger to big waves that missed him. By contrast, Jim Kilroy speaks of the need to flow with a storm, comparing it to the way in which one uses one's opponent's momentum to throw him in a judo contest.

That notion had more appeal for Fingers. He thought it was misguided of people to take natural events personally. He wasn't one openly to combat a force like the sea, or take its unpredictable moods lightly. After the legend provided by Melville, Conrad, Coleridge, and others, and after a few thousand miles of water had passed under one's own keel, there could be no forgiveness for arrogance. Bad karma is

not a good shipmate. Sailors with any sense yield before the sea, tread softly upon its shores as a show of
respect and humility that they hope, in their childlike
way, will solicit a bit of protection when they are at
its mercy.

Once Fingers had lived on a Navy barge off
Bermuda for two weeks in the course of covering an
underwater habitat project. At least twice a day he
had to swim a hundred yards from the barge to a diving platform. Each time, a couple dozen barracuda
would detach themselves from the main body of the
thousand or so that were stacked up like cordwood
in the shade of the barge, feeding on garbage, and
follow him across, trailing lazily ten feet behind his
flippers. Their ability to accelerate suddenly, with a
little wiggle, reminded him of cats.

The support divers on the project had been
commandeered from all over. They were the best the
Navy had. None of them had ever seen a barracuda
attack a man. By continually reminding himself of
that fact, Fingers was able to keep making the swim.
But then one day he found himself with one of the
more macho divers, who carried his spear gun into
the thick of the barracuda. As he watched, horrified,
the man calmly surveyed them, picked out the biggest
one, and shot it at point-blank range. Talk about bad
karma. He wanted to scream at the guy, Lenny Bruce
style, "Come on, man, I've got to do business with
these assholes!" He kept swimming every day, but
after that incident he felt like fair game.

Preparation must follow respect. Skills and experience must be matched with proper gear and a stout vessel worthy of what the elements might provide. Readiness is relative. For cruising in the ocean one considers the strength and seaworthiness of the vessel, the degree of comfort it will provide, water and fuel capacity, the ease of handling the sails, and the privacy it affords below. If the boat is responsive and fast, so much the better.

Racing on the ocean is another matter. The nature of all racing is to explore limits. Ocean racing used to be a rather sedate sport. Rigorous, but social. Get a good strong boat with pleasant accommodations that showed decent speed by comparison to its peers, fit it with good sails, collect a bunch of compatible mates, some good food, and a few bottles of hootch with which to acknowledge sunsets, and off you would go, blow ye winds hi ho.

Not any more. Today's ocean racers are temperamental thoroughbreds that are as carefully engineered and as full of technological innovation as any space capsule. Super Boats. Speed, factored into a marvelously complex, sixty-two-page mathematical handicapping formula called the International Ocean Racing (IOR) Rule, is the overriding consideration. New limits that have been devised by computer application are being tested. New designs that take advantage of rule modifications give boats less displacement, more speed. New materials like Kevlar and carbon fiber for hull and rigging produce boats that are lighter, faster. Innovations like hydraulic applications make heavy load adjustments easier, more precise, faster. New electronic devices like satellite navigation systems, weather facsimile machines, and mini-processors make navigation areas look like the cockpits of passenger jets. And new construction techniques not only take weight out of the ends of boats, thus reducing their tendency to pitch, but put the center of gravity within inches of where it will be most effective for maximum speed. Sailmaking is now a fully computerized business, and no season passes without the introduction of a new thread, a better weaving system, a new coating, or an entirely new fabric—not to mention the continuous introduction of new aerodynamic theories, new shapes; "the shape of speed," as one sailmaker dubs his product. Phrases like "performance envelope" that were once reserved for describing the capabilities of the most sophisticated state-of-the-the-art jet aircraft are creeping into the language of grand-prix Super Boats.

Strength and seaworthiness are still important, because a boat that falls apart cannot win, and the need to win that has infected all sports ("we're number one!") is what has liberated the millions of dollars it has taken to finance the development of the Super Boats. But comfort is definitely an afterthought, privacy doesn't exist, and there is no cocktail hour on most boats. "Do you think we are out here to have fun?" is no longer a good joke. And safety? Well, safety is a moot point.

Ocean-racing gear is strong and well-conceived in general, and safety considerations are adequate. But safety is mainly a state of mind. Is a race driver's primary thought as he is strapped into his car for the Big One that he is going to drive safely? Speed and safety have never been very compatible. There are many ways to kill yourself in the name of sport. To win at most sports one must be willing to hang it out, take it to the limit. Ocean racing is no different.

The new technology of sailing has given rise to the businesslike, systematized approach to winning as practiced by big businessmen who have become rich enough to enter the game in the first place. Super Boats aren't designed, built, and raced; they are "organized." Organization is the name of the Super Boat chess game. Money, computers, and expertise are the pieces. Just like at the office.

The result of all this money and organization is that the top twenty or forty Super Boats in any present-day ocean race are all potential winners. On these boats, the best crews have been organized – many of them professionals – and naturally the best sails have been obtained. And the tactics for most ocean races have been standardized to an amazing degree. In 1979's Transatlantic Race, for instance, after four days of sailing, *Kialoa* and *Condor* came out of a fog bank in mid-ocean on opposite tacks within ten boat lengths of one another. The racing is that close.

What remains in the way of achieving an edge is to hang it out further than the next guy. Running aground, for instance, used to be called bad seamanship. These days it is an indication of how hard one is trying to win. In one of the Admiral's Cup races which preceded the Fastnet Race, half the fleet of fifty-seven boats scraped their keels against rocks in their efforts to stay furthest inshore of a foul current. The same thing happened in the early stages of the Fastnet. And that's not all. It got hairier, as we shall see.

Winning, as a concept, has never been quite so important. Here, at the highest level of a very expensive sport, the captains of industry play hard. With money only a passing consideration, the game is to find out what else and how much one is willing to give up. Because the more one is willing to give up – in terms of time, energy, other interests, even family, friends, and sometimes basic humanity – the more one can win. At this level of competition in any endeavor, the alternative to winning is not losing. The alternative to winning is living. As we shall see.

If Fingers had one moment of fear (anticipation of danger) during the whole Fastnet experience it was the day of the race itself when he stepped aboard *Kialoa* for the first time. He stood on the immense expanse of deck taking in just the major elements and he was stunned, rooted to the spot by the sheer size of it all. This was big. Frighteningly big. The Biggest. Maxi Boat.

Fingers is a Sunfish racer by choice. He has raced on some forty-footers, even a sixty-footer, but he likes Sunfish best. Aside from that almost-in-the-water feeling of intimacy with the elements the little boats provide, there is a sense of full control that is reassuring. One man, one boat, one sail. The larger a boat gets, the less physical control of it any one person can have. At first glance, there didn't look like anything on *Kialoa* that one average-size person could move without help. At first glance *Kialoa* made sixty-footers—even twelve-meters—look manageable by comparison.

There is a little dance that new crew members do when they go aboard a strange yacht for the first time. It could be choreographed, like the dance of a batter in the on-deck circle, or a basketball player at the foul line. It is called Taking It All In, and consists of a stroll around the deck checking out where things are and how they work. Usually the dance is done with other crew members hovering, and it therefore becomes something of a rite of evaluation and acceptance (or rejection) of the new man. A senior crew member will often trail the new man around, keeping a proper distance, of course, letting him set the pace, but close enough to answer questions and maybe work in a piece or two of general boat operational policy.

It is a dance best done with light feet. The new man wants to exude confidence but not arrogance. He wants to establish a few credits—appear knowledgeable—but not to the point of alienating the others. He also needs information. If he sees a piece of gear or a system that puzzles him, he'd better ask about it. But of course too many questions will arouse doubts about his experience, his worth.

Fingers had to work at keeping his jaw from dropping over the size (five-eighths of an inch diameter) and tension (nearly immobile) of the triple solid-rod stainless rigging that lasered skyward ninety-five feet to the mast tip. The forestay and shrouds had been tested to sixty thousand pounds. The backstay, he was told by his minder, would often be loaded to fourteen thousand pounds. The mast section was 14.75 inches by 8.9 inches at the base. The six wire halyards, spliced into three-quarter-inch braided Dacron tails and clipped to a bridle at the front of the mast, had snap shackles as big as the palm of his hand. Their two-speed winches were the biggest that could be turned by a single handle. The hydraulic vang for holding the boom down was a seven-foot long, three-inch metal cylinder. He would become especially fond of the vang. The distance from the mast to the tip of the bow seemed of tennis-court proportions. Along it, on either side, lay the twin spinnaker poles in their brackets. The poles were twenty-nine-and-a-half foot, seven-inch aluminum tubes that, with hardware, weighed one hundred fifty pounds each. Work was in progress here. Four men were straining over one of the smaller jibs—dry weight one hundred fifty pounds—folding it into a turtle (quick release bag).

Back aft, the captain handed Fingers a *Kialoa* T-shirt. The shirts are passed out to all crew before every major race. Delighted, Fingers shook the shirt out and looked at it. It was an extra large, the only size Kilroy orders—the final intimidation. Fingers was pleased to hear a crewman who outweighed him by thirty pounds wryly suggest that the huge shirts had been ordered from Omar the tent maker.

A Maxi Boat is the largest boat that can race under the IOR Rule without special dispensations. When a boat rates around 67, 68, or, in *Kialoa*'s case 69.6, it is called Maxi.

Kialoa is Jim Kilroy's third ocean racer. He started with a fifty-foot yawl in 1962, moved on to a seventy-three-foot sloop in 1964, and built the present boat in 1974. It was designed by the New York yacht design firm of Sparkman & Stephens, with David Pedrick directing the project. The Palmer-Johnson yard in Michigan built her of aluminum. Pedrick, as much as anyone, can lay claim to *Kialoa*'s design. He formulated the boat's concept, drew the lines, played an integral part in the initial sea trials, and did extensive design modification on the boat after he left Sparkman & Stephens. Pedrick, in turn, passes a generous share of the credit for the boat to Kilroy and his main man, Bruce Kendall. They asked for a wider boat with less displacement than the one Pedrick had drawn. Pedrick did the calculations and found that their intuition was right. Basically, Pedrick says, the boat was designed with rough water in mind, as a sea-kindly ocean boat, not a smooth-water flier.

Kialoa began, of course, with Jim Kilroy, one of the small handful of men in the whole world who want Maxi Boats. In the fall of 1979, there were twelve new Maxis under consideration worldwide. Some of them wouldn't make it through the design stage, but even so, that was more Maxi thinking than ever before. To many men with Kilroy's money, his energy and drive, perhaps even his talent as a seaman, having a Maxi Boat is like having a whole business on the side, and most businessmen don't need that.

The initial investment is huge. The present *Kialoa* cost around seven hundred fifty thousand dollars to design and build. The new *Kialoa* that Kilroy hopes to have in the water by December 1980, will cost more than one million dollars. Sails alone will run one hundred thousand dollars. And that is only the beginning of what one crewman calls the *Kialoa* Industrial Complex.

A Maxi Boat doesn't just sit at a mooring in front of one's summer home. A full-time captain and a paid crew of four men work day and night on operational and cosmetic maintenance. This complement of five live on the boat, and also are constantly en route, delivering the boat from the finish of one race (in Australia, for example) to the start of another (perhaps in Florida). Then there is Bruce Kendall, who is employed full time by Kilroy Industries, and whose main job is supervising and coordinating *Kialoa* operations. With a new boat in the design stage, and an old boat to sell, Kendall usually works a ten-hour day at the office when he isn't sailing. Add food, provisions, hotels, and air fares; new sails (spinnakers cost eight thousand dollars, new headsails six to seven thousand dollars apiece); yard bills; electronic and mechanical maintenance; and general maintenance. A small item: those six halyards cost four hundred dollars each, and they should be replaced every six months or so.

Kilroy also uses the boat for cruising. Typically, after one race or another, all the racing sails and gear will be loaded into a container which will be air-freighted to the site of the next race. Then the cruising container, which has been air-freighted in, will be unloaded onto the boat: diving gear, inflatable dinghies, outboard motors, cruising sails, wine, gourmet food, and various items of creature comfort that have been sacrificed in the interest of keeping the boat light for racing. Then friends will appear, and Mrs. Kilroy, and off they will go for a month in the Pacific, or some other warm-water version of paradise.

On the average, it costs Kilroy about three hundred thousand dollars a year to enjoy his Maxi Boat—if no modifications are done that year. And in the Super Boat game, modifications have become common. It is another way of hanging it out. The IOR Rule is altered constantly, if subtly, and new hot boats are being launched all the time. If one wants to stay competitive between boats, he needs more than new sails. He needs to keep getting the most out of the rule. He needs perhaps to reshape the bow, change the size of the keel, get a more flexible mast, or add more hydraulic systems. These are major changes, expensive ones, and they don't always work (hang it out!). Because the designers and the engineers continually plunge back into the capacious IOR formula, where they wander for days among the forest of numbers, considering exotic new materials and techniques, with the owner pressing them for results—rarely with helpful suggestions— and sometimes in their acrobatic efforts to squeeze one last small increment of speed out of the yacht, a performance result will occasionally be achieved that is akin to putting oval wheels on a bicycle.

Kialoa had been doing just fine in the ocean. Over the two-year period 1975-77, it had won the World Ocean Racing Championship for having the best combined record over a prescribed set of races. It never finished worse than second. But in 1977, it began competing in round-the-buoys events—closed-course races—and didn't fare so well. Other boats began beating it. That would never do. So Dave Pedrick redesigned her keel, enlarging it and moving it aft. The rudder was moved aft and the afterbody shape altered. Major surgery. Then the rig was changed. From a ketch (with two masts) she became a sloop. That meant a new mast, of course, a new boom, new rigging (a seventy thousand dollar order), and a new sail inventory. The *Kialoa* Industrial Complex!

The work was done at a yard in New Zealand, with Bruce Kendall supervising and *Kialoa*'s own versatile crew providing most of the work force. Even so, that year had to cost Kilroy in excess of five hundred thousand dollars. But it was worth it. *Kialoa* came out of the hospital a much faster, livelier boat.

In the case of *Kialoa*, there was never much worry over whether or not the extensive modifications would work. Pedrick knew the boat intimately, and he is a cautious, thoughtful man, an excellent engineer. But mainly Jim Kilroy was on top of it. Pedrick would have to show Kilroy the numbers, prove his calculations, argue his case with a man who really knows the score about such things. Because Jim Kilroy is smart, efficient, jammed with energy, driven, a mathematical wizard with a background in aeronautics from an early stint he did in that industry, and later in the Air Force. He knows the numbers. He understands things like hydrostatic and seismic loading. And he is a man with a consuming passion to be Right.

"If he has a weakness," his son John Kilroy, Jr., says, "it is that he tries to be too right; he has to rationalize in his mind that he is right."

But Jim Kilroy is Right! He has a record to prove it. Albeit with some frustration, John Jr., who says he is his father's greatest fan and greatest critic, has to admit it: "He thinks he knows everything . . . and he pretty much does."

As the little magnetic program cards zip through his H-P calculator, Jim Kilroy taps away at the buttons and can tell you everything from why he doesn't use inset windows in the office buildings he puts up – not only because they would form natural perches for pigeons, but they would reduce the inside space by six inches on each side, and that would amount to one foot total, or the loss of two hundred square feet per floor times ten floors at thirteen dollars per square foot, or forty thousand five hundred dollars per year in rent! – to why *Kialoa*'s keel had to be enlarged by twenty square feet to take an excess of hydrostatic loading off the hull.

In the fall of 1979, Kilroy flew into Dulles Airport in Washington from London. He strode briskly off a plane that was five hours late in a terrific mood, lean and alert. He looked outstanding in sparkling white flannel trousers, with a soft butterscotch leather jacket by Hermès of Paris over an emerald green chemise Lacoste that set off his snow-white hair and the elegant tan he had picked up cruising for six weeks in the Med. In the restaurant he could hardly wait to order a scotch and a cheeseburger before grabbing a napkin and drawing sketches of boats as he explained why the new *Kialoa* would not be built of the latest in Kevlar-carbon fiber combinations. The new material would not save 25 percent in weight, as the potential builder claimed. He had done the calculations. The new material hadn't been sufficiently tested. Close friends in the aircraft industry had told him that while the F-18 fuselage was indeed being constructed of the new material, a "clean room" environment was essential for good bonding. And even then it was a bitch.

As soon as possible he hauled out a below-decks plan and a deck plan for the new boat that had obviously taken up the lion's share of his alleged vacation. "My father's idea of relaxation," John Jr. has said, "is to go full speed in another direction."

Kilroy went over both plans in full detail, and with obvious relish at some of the innovations and concepts. He told how he had gotten the crew involved, listened to their ideas about winch placement, sail stowage techniques, etc. "Now that they can say 'I was involved,' they'll try harder to make it work," Kilroy said. "I don't want zombies around me, I want people who think. They will have to perform by the numbers eventually, decisions will have to be unilateral in the end, but I try never to make it a matter of pride versus pride. Take away a person's pride and you have a terrible problem."

The following day Kilroy met with Gary Carlin and Fang Kilponen of Kiwi Boats to talk about building the new *Kialoa*. Having rehearsed his rap on more innocent parties, Kilroy laid out his plans, ideas, misgivings, and proposals, right down to the hiring of the work force and the division of other responsibilities. It wasn't exactly what Carlin and Kilponen had in mind, but it was acceptable.

"Jim has done his homework," Fang said. "I still think we could save him twenty-five percent of the weight. But he isn't the guy to be first with something this new. And the amount of research he has done is impressive."

The deal they struck was complex. Kiwi would build the boat, but Kilroy would supply most of the work force. Construction of the hull and deck would be a combination of Kiwi's exotic materials and aluminum. Purchasing and overall supervision would be by Kiwi. The profit margin would be fixed. The new *Kialoa* would be Kiwi's biggest undertaking. The status factor wouldn't be bad, either.

"There probably isn't anyone else we would make such a deal with," Fang said. "But Jim and I have had a long association. He is knowledgeable, and we can do business with him."

Kilroy went shopping for accessories at the world's largest in-the-water boat show, then in progress in Annapolis, Maryland. At Brooks and Gatehouse, a well-known manufacturer of electronic instruments (wind speed, direction, boat speed, etc.), Kilroy gave the gentleman manning the booth a short lecture on why they should redesign the little plastic impeller on their boat-speed underwater hull fitting. He stopped at Barient and at Lewmar, telling each group of winch makers about the new boat. He said he would send them a deck plan and would expect bids. The guys from Lewmar were one step away from openly drooling as they listened to Kilroy describe a winch order in the neighborhood of sixty thousand dollars.

He stopped at Hood Yacht Systems and Sterns Sailing Systems to solicit bids on mast and rigging. Tim Sterns began talking about exotic hydraulic applications. Kilroy shrugged, said he would consider them, but mainly he wanted everything delivered and ready to install in Florida by August—with a written guarantee of performance. Yes, sir!

Even at the world's largest in-the-water boat show the Presence had been felt. Among the hundreds of strollers and boat gawkers and dreamers and young couples thinking about that little day sailer or maybe a new outboard for the old scow, here was a man bent on doing business, Big Business, Maxi Boat Business. The White Tornado was taking the show by storm. Even the folks selling the sweaters and boat shoes or the framed boating prints or bikinis out of little booths looked up, felt the charge of energy as this six-foot-four-inch Maxi Man went by, the half smile upon his lips, the intense blue eyes piercing out of the tanned, raw-boned, handsome face, the white hair like a bobbing masthead light in the crowd. Those who had no idea who he was knew he was Somebody.

Jim Kilroy was born in Alaska in 1922. He still has a photograph of himself, aged six months, bundled into a dog sled. His mother is standing beside him with an Eskimo guide. They were about to take off on a six-hundred-mile trip into the interior to meet his father.

Kilroy's mother was born in South Dakota. Her father died when she was six. So her mother picked up the family and moved to Alaska, then as now a land of opportunity. There Jim's mother met his father, a prospector, a soldier of fortune, a gambler, and a drinker who had been born in a cabin in Schull, Ireland, in the shadow of Fastnet Rock. She once walked forty miles to have one of her three babies.

Jim's father discovered what turned out to be a substantial gold mine. He lost it in a poker game before it was even registered. The family drifted south to Los Angeles by way of San Francisco, Montana, Tucson, and Phoenix. They settled in the run-down Southgate section. When Jim was nine, his father went to New York on business. He never returned.

Hard times. It was the height of the Depression. Jim's mother worked nights at a newspaper job. Jim and his brother scrounged for money. By his early teens, Jim was big enough to lie about his age. Eating was important, so he went after jobs associated with food. Washing dishes in restaurants, stocking shelves in supermarkets. He had a good memory even then and was promoted to checker because he knew the prices. But in southern California, even in hard times, the sun keeps shining almost every day, and there is always the beach. Like most southern California kids, Kilroy managed to get in his share of beach time, surfing, and water sports. He had his first sail as a result of a contest he won as a newsboy. Part of the prize was a trip to Balboa and a day spent on small boats.

In high school Jim excelled at track and basketball. He set a record in the high hurdles that stood until former Los Angeles Rams' halfback Hugh McElhenny broke it. He was a good enough basketball player to play semipro and later for the Air Force. His athletic ability got him a college scholarship, but there still wasn't enough money to make up the difference. He dropped out and went back to work.

He had the first of two unannounced visits from his father while in college. "I couldn't get mad at him," Jim recalls. "He was my father. And he always was a charmer. I felt no resentment toward him. His behavior probably made me more self-reliant. Thanks to him I made up my mind about one thing: I was never going to be poor."

When World War II broke out, Jim found himself working at Douglas Aircraft as an inspector. He was one of a number of people his age working at the frantic pace of war production and taking aeronautics courses on the side to keep up with a burgeoning industry. Jim met his first wife at Douglas. She was a former homecoming queen. The homecoming queen and the athlete.

Jim's desire to be a chemistry or physics professor came to an end at Douglas. As shop organization would have it, he had some professors working on his crew. He saw their paychecks. They were making less than he was. As an inspector he had a chance to observe the plants of subcontractors. He became fascinated with the layouts and designs of various industrial facilities and how they could make working life more or less difficult, more or less productive. "I learned in those days," Kilroy says, "that if you traded a reflecting pool for a good toilet facility, you came out ahead." It was a thought that stayed with him after the war, when it was time to figure out what he might do.

He predicted big growth for southern California. The war had built the aircraft industry into a many-headed monster, and all the heads were located in southern California: Northrop, Convair, Douglas, Rockwell, Lockheed, Hughes, etc. Others thought southern California would become a ghost town, that everyone would go home after the war. Kilroy saw Americans migrating over the world. He saw a great communications network, people traveling by air, southerners going west, midwesterners going south; a liberated mentality. He couldn't imagine a person stationed in sunny California wanting to go home after the war to Podunk, to ice and snow.

He didn't see big money to be made in consumer goods right away, but as the war wore down, manufacturing of new equipment and tools that were by-products of war technology would begin. Warehousing and distribution plants would come first. Then manufacturing facilities would be needed. And office space.

First he sold insurance. He discovered his talent as a salesman, cracking the million-dollar club the first year. Then he moved on into a small real-estate company. By the late 1940s he had a plan. He figured he could build and lease a facility for about the same price a tenant could find existing space. The key was to find a tenant with good credit who was willing to sign a lease in advance of construction. With lease in hand, he could borrow the money, put the package together, build the building, sell it for a profit, and finance the next deal himself. And that is what he did.

In 1950 Kilroy made his first really big move. He bid on a sixty-acre parcel of land on which he planned to build his first industrial park. His was not the winning bid, but he became a partner of the man who bought it. Together they put up a million and a half square feet of space on the sixty acres, and leased it all within thirteen months. Kilroy was the general contractor, real-estate broker, and part owner. The deal put Kilroy into a whole new league.

Kilroy erects office towers like he builds a new boat, or vice versa. He uses architects, literally uses them. Their numbers better match his. They have to work hard to come up with ideas that are better than

Kilroy's, that use space more efficiently. Kilroy has given the greatest attention to the details of telephone and electrical cabinets, elevator shafts, toilet facilities: the critical nonrentable space. No inset windows! He feels he is from 2 to 5 percent more efficient in the planning of these spaces, which in industrial real estate is a considerable margin.

To Kilroy, his ownership of buildings is important. It means a better building that will attract a higher-caliber tenant who is willing to pay a little more for a quality product. Some of Kilroy's tenants have been with him for thirty years. He likes to acquire buildings he once sold. Recently he purchased a tower he built for the Jewel Tea Company in 1959. It cost nine hundred thousand dollars at the time. He bought it back for two million seven hundred thousand dollars, completely renovated it, and leased it.

Working out of his Los Angeles headquarters in the Kilroy Airport Center—dual brown-tinted glass towers and a huge (twenty-five hundred car) parking garage within five minutes of the Los Angeles Airport—Kilroy commands a substantial empire. Kilroy Industries puts the deals together. The John B. Kilroy Company handles the brokerage. There is a corporate office in New York, and a new office in Seattle. Since he started, Jim Kilroy has built more than sixty million square feet of industrial real estate, retaining ownership of approximately 10 percent of it. His is a privately owned company, and Kilroy isn't one to talk about his money. John Jr., who is vice-president-marketing, put it in understated perspective. "If we were to merge with a hundred-million-dollar company," he said, "we would survive."

Jim's second and last visit from his father occurred in 1960. An old man came into the office saying that his name was Kilroy. The secretary tried to move him along. He wouldn't budge, and finally charmed her with hastily scribbled poems. "He was in his nineties," Jim says. "He wanted a dictation machine so he could record his memoirs." He was broke, of course, so Kilroy gave his father some cash. The old man took the money and threw a party. It was a good one, culminating in his fall from a second-story window. He languished in the hospital for two days before he died.

Jim Kilroy has an appreciation that borders on wistfulness for the romantic, carefree gambler's life his father lived. "He fought in the Boer War," he will say, dropping that fact with a grin of obvious pride. One of the first things Kilroy tells a stranger is that he was born in Alaska. If he thinks it was missed, he might repeat it. Before the start of the Fastnet Race, he spent a week cruising in Ireland on a sort of "roots" trip, hanging around Schull, digging into family history. But any paternal reminiscence is inevitably capped with a light disclaimer, "his life was a fantasy . . . the real world was too much for him." In other words, it was a great gig, but it didn't work. And Jim Kilroy is passionately dedicated to what works. His life has been devoted to the study of it. Workology.

What works, Kilroy has decided, is Controlled Averages, and that is about as far from the romantic as one can steer. Controlled Averages, two powerful words that in Kilroy Newspeak have a frightening ring because of their unmistakable fail-safe connotation. Controlled Averages. It sounds like a system that ought to be illegal, like goal tending in basketball.

The concept involves soliciting maximum input from employees. "I give them an objective and outline the game plan," Kilroy says. "But I want their execution of it to be operable within their personal styles in order to get the performance we want. I can't ask other people to be me, or do it my way. There are many different approaches, and I learn from all of them. So in the end what we have is a 'directed collective' of people, bracketed within a stated objective, and of course a unilateral decision at the end. You create an organization, and then let the organization do it. Fine-tune it, but keep your thumbs out of it."

Since Kilroy is the one doing the directing of the collective, it is useful to look at what he expects from himself. He gets up at seven, has a run with his golden retriever, makes his own coffee and juice, eats breakfast alone, and thinks. He is in the office at 9:30 and gets directly to work, having been "fine-tuned" over breakfast. He reads the mail, and he may make a call or two, but accepts no calls or appointments until 10:30.

He is a firm believer in what the subconscious mind can do. After each meeting or phone call, he makes a few notes in summation, thinking the situation through once more, then "enters" the information in his subconscious. The ultimate H-P. The entry is dated, and also specifies a date by which action will be taken. If necessary, he writes a short memo to the staff asking them for comment. He asks his secretary to give the pertinent information back to him on a certain date.

He doesn't mull over the problem. There is no need. "Why waste conscious time? The greatest possible brain power is at work on it!" On decision day he will invariably know his mind.

Every staffer's appointment with Kilroy must be preceded by a handwritten memo of purpose. Handwritten so that not even a word will be altered in deference to secretarial eyes. And memos tend to be shorter handwritten. "The memo brings me up to speed," Kilroy says. "And the staffer has articulated the problem to himself, gotten the subconscious going. People think more about what they are saying on paper than aloud." Controlled Averages.

When business slows down at 6 p.m., Kilroy has more quiet time, reviewing the day, cleaning his desk (without fail), loading up the old subconscious data banks. When he leaves at 7:30, he swears his business problems do not go with him.

Kilroy is as concerned about his employees' physical well-being as he is about them having a well-oiled subconscious. Because he believes in the value of stress. The only time he is apprehensive, he says, is when nothing is happening, when there is nothing to react to. He is very aware of his own physical self. He runs. He plays a lot of tennis. If the need arose, he could probably handle, physically, most of the brawny crewmen who sail on *Kialoa*. At the clinic of Dr. Toby Friedman, who supervises the training of the Los Angeles Rams and Dodgers athletic teams, Kilroy has been weighed in water to determine the percentage of fat in his body. After a rigorous series of tests over a three-day period, Friedman designed a specific exercise program for him.

Kilroy has sent every one of his executives through the program. "I believe people work better under pressure," Kilroy says. "And I want to know how much they can take."

Kilroy was giving Fingers problems. On the one hand he not only thought Kilroy was a pretty good guy, but he also admired him. Behind Fingers' modified 1960s street-kid appearance was a strong affinity for systems. He had made his own study of what worked, and liked to act accordingly. He had systems for everything from doing dishes to rigging his Sunfish to stacking firewood. In that way he could relate to Kilroy and the H-P on his hip. But unlike Kilroy, Fingers had confined the systems to the less significant parts of his life. It would have been overly constricting in his line of work to use too many systems. Especially when the only company he had to run was a one-man operation. It was necessary to be very careful, in a one-man operation, to keep the janitor and the guy in research and development on the most cordial terms with the production and financial vice-presidents. They all spent far too much time together for any social or business system in the world to work. One had to ad lib all the time. There was another difference. Fingers knew that even with diligent employment of systems in the lower echelons of his life, he was fighting a losing battle. Kilroy had more confidence in his systems. He knew he was winning. He had the numbers to prove it. He was used to winning, not desperate about it; for him it was a way of life.

Fingers had to credit Kilroy for the way he hung it out with the rest of the guys. Most men of fifty-seven who have made the kind of money Kilroy has tend to retreat a bit, add another foot to the walls around their estate, turn up the indoor pool heat a notch, see who they want to see when they want to see them. Not Kilroy. One could count on the fingers of one hand the races he had missed over the last ten years. He was always at the helm for the start, did his share of driving even in the worst weather, and had a strong and productive voice in all major decisions, tactical and otherwise. He shared his master cabin with two crewmen, and asked for nothing more in the way of special privilege than that an occasional cup of Sanka be brought to him at the wheel. On the boat he became just another ocean-racing crazy, hanging it out there, revealing himself under all conditions for all to see. And what he revealed was mostly admirable. There wasn't a guy on the boat who didn't have high regard for him.

During the Fastnet storm when he got his ribs

busted, his main response was bitter disappointment at having to go below. But he did so with dignity befitting an officer and a gentleman. He could have railed against the two men who fell on him, but he didn't. He could have carried on below, but he didn't. After he was helped into his bunk and bedded down with a pain-killer he said thank you, and yes he was comfortable, no problem, and he got out a book and read his way back to England when he wasn't sleeping.

Kilroy wasn't the most popular guy in the ocean-racing circuit, Fingers had gathered that. Not that popularity accounted for much in a competitive endeavor of grand-prix caliber. But people had spoken of his propensity for the grand posture, posing at the helm, his need for good public relations for himself and the boat, his egomania. Others criticized him for having fun mucking around with too many little race meetings (like Antigua Race Week) when he should be out there going after Flying Cloud's New York-San Francisco record. A former *Kialoa* crewman may have gotten to the heart of it. "I can't stand him," the guy said, "but I admire him. Hey, if I had the money, guess what I would be doing? It's sick, but try me. Kilroy isn't an easy guy to like. Why? Because he is doing what a hell of a lot of us would like to be doing. So eat your heart out."

One thing that had endeared Kilroy to Fingers was his attitude about the New York Yacht Club, that stuffy Manhattan bastion of self-aggrandizing Yachting Power. "No," Kilroy answered when Fingers asked him if he belonged to the club. "I've never been able to understand why I should. Frankly I would rather have my name on their trophies than on their membership list." His smile was one of satisfaction.

But then Kilroy could follow up that deft put-down, that heartwarming, patently West Coast signifier, with a line about how he sent all his executives to the health clinic in the interest of seeing how much they could take – just how far he would be able to push them, in other words, in the interest of productivity, that sounded absolutely brutal. Fingers was having problems with that. Not long after all the folks had worked themselves into a state of near collapse for the good Dr. Toby Friedman, a truck pulled up at Kilroy Industries and began unloading large cardboard boxes – enough for everyone. Gifts from Jim, at a hundred and twenty dollars each. Inside each was a device called the Aero Tram Jogger, a thirty-by-forty-inch trampoline upon which a vigorous six-minute run in place was equal to a mile on the cinder track. One of the trampolines still sits outside Jim's office. No others are in sight. A good way to inhibit conversation with a KI executive is to inquire about the trampolines. The little Aero Tram Joggers were just too much. One step over the line.

Fingers' problems with Kilroy ranged from pity to anger to pure amazement. How, he wondered, could a serious fan of Clint Eastwood like himself feel at all comfortable fraternizing with a totally self-conscious man for whom relaxation was so impossible, for whom a little humorous banter was so difficult to dredge up; whose incredible drive, energy, and focused concentration never let up; who admitted to a consuming cleanliness fetish supported by a veritable traveling storehouse of lotions, emollients, and powders that made clean sheets on bunks and sterile feet important issues even during the Fastnet storm (sterile feet?); who avowed that smog in Los Angeles was caused more by the carbon monoxide given off by the plants in people's gardens and the evaporation of salt crystals from the ocean than by automobile exhaust; who would have turned fire hoses on the rebellious students of the 1960s without a second thought; who thought that the Pope, for all his sexist views and his adamant refusal to grant the blessing of birth control to impoverished, disease-racked, overpopulated countries, was the greatest; who was a high-ranking official of Southern California Republicans for John Connally; who was a substantial financial backer and continued to be devoted follower of one Richard M. Nixon. The enormity of it made Fingers shake his head in some frustration. Why wasn't this guy a write-off?

Then Fingers ran into his old friend Warwick Tompkins, a man known since his infancy as Commodore. As a sailor Tompkins was one of the best. He sailed across the Atlantic aboard his father's North Sea pilot schooner when he was two weeks old. When he was four, he rounded Cape Horn with his old man at the helm. As a sailor he was more adept at ten than most men ever become, and over the years he has gotten better.

Tompkins used to work for Kilroy. He was captain of the first big boat, a fifty-foot yawl that the previous owner had named *Kialoa*, a Hawaiian word meaning "long white canoe." Tompkins says Kilroy was a good employer. He recalls he had a generous way about him. He often made suggestions to Tompkins about real-estate investments.

In 1964, when Kilroy decided to build his first Maxi Boat, Tompkins was to stay on as captain and supervise construction. The only problem was that the boat was scheduled to be built at Douglas Aircraft. That was a problem because security was very tight at Douglas at the time, and, well, Commodore's old man, Warwick, Sr., had been an outspoken member of the Communist Party most of his life. Because of that, Commodore was never going to get security clearance. He told Kilroy.

Kilroy came on like a dutch uncle. He told Tompkins that he had friends in government, in intelligence work, and that he could arrange for Tompkins to make a statement dissociating himself from his father, sign some papers, and make a clean breast of it.

Commodore had never shared his father's political views. While he had followed him as a sailor, his overall regard for his father was perhaps slightly below the national average for that of sons for fathers. But Tompkins was offended by Kilroy's suggestion. He thought it was a real bad suggestion. He remembers having an instant image of a Hitler Youth kid moving himself up the ladder by turning in his own family for disloyalty.

But Tompkins took the suggestion calmly. And he was glad he did. "Jim really meant well," Tompkins says. "He really meant to make it better for me. He did me a great favor, unintentionally. He taught me that a man could have an evil idea with the best intentions. It blew the demonology theory: evil idea, therefore evil man.

"His error, if any, was his failure to perceive what kind of person I was. He suggested a course that would have sunk my operation. My father and I weren't close, but even so I couldn't have cut myself adrift. Maybe he has been adrift, maybe that's why it didn't occur to him.

"As an individual he is strange," Tompkins says. "There is something about him. He is the difference between an old brick oven and a microwave."

A microwave! Perfect. The Brick Oven and the Microwave. Fingers could relate to that.

Jim Kilroy *was* cut adrift, as we have seen, which is enough to account for the emphasis he places on his nuclear family. Not just with the strong ties he works hard to keep secured with his own five children, a family scene complicated once by divorce, but with the greater family, the *Kialoa* Family—some fifty crewmen strong who have been part of the Big Run for the Silver that began in 1964 with the seventy-three-foot yawl.

For a man with Kilroy's drive, expertise, desire to be in the forefront of whatever he does, his organizational ability (Controlled Averages), and his ingrained and thorough confidence in his ability to achieve his goals, it was predictable that it would work, from the design selection and technology (after real-estate and construction deals usually running to fifty million dollars, how difficult could that be) to the assemblage of a first-rate crew. Because, as Fingers would attest, Jim Kilroy is an OK guy to sail with.

As the brightest stars of the most glittering fleet, the Maxi Boats are never short of crew applicants. They are irresistible to any sailor. They are the tallest, the sleekest, the fastest, and the most comfortable, the most spectacularly powerful, the most breathtaking, the most beautiful, and the most photogenic. Their passing, with flawless sails in perfect trim, with all forces coordinated in a delicious-sounding sensual surge of speed—eighty thousand pounds of displaced water wedged against a glass-smooth hull; Dacron and steel wire straining evenly against aluminum—is the most magnificent. They are the most seductive. Their wakes are the creamiest. What sailor could honestly say he wouldn't give a nickel to sail on a Maxi Boat?

But Maxi Boats need more than enthusiastic crewmen. Maxi Boats need the very best crewmen. On a Maxi Boat, even the smallest adjustment made inadvertently, or at the wrong time, could cause a disaster. Things could break, rip, tear, people could get hurt. The loads are awesome. With one man hauling on the line as it comes off the winch (tailing), it takes another man of more than average brawn on the winch handle, putting out 100-percent effort, to manage half a turn at a time in order to increase main halyard tension. Many jobs on the boat involve three or more men coordinating their efforts like riggers moving heavy machinery. When you are one of the three, your life and limbs depend on the worth of the other two. That a person is competent is the least that one wishes to say about a fellow crewman on a Maxi Boat.

The greatest single factor inhibiting the assembly of a top crew on any boat is the owner. Boats, like the money that buys them, don't care who owns them. In fact, there have been so many famously obnoxious owners in the sport that owners in general are undeservedly considered guilty until proved innocent. Live lobsters in the bilge are just the beginning. Any well-traveled sailor's list of owner atrocities would fill a notebook. No boat, even a Maxi Boat, is worth putting up with a man who habitually comes below and stretches out on one of the two available dining table settees and lights up a fat cigar as the off-watch is about to have chow—just to let everybody know who holds all the cards.

Kialoa has never had crew problems. That is partly because Kilroy is a good sailor himself, and he is totally involved in all facets of the boat. He is a proven winner, and that does a lot to attract crew. And he doesn't smoke cigars. Mainly *Kialoa* is well staffed because Kilroy has not only decided to live the Big Dream himself, but he has made it available to others. He has had to. For one thing, the Big Dream is too much even for a Maxi Man to pull off alone. But sharing it is his pleasure as well. Sharing the Big Dream is right up his alley. Controlled Averages.

Kialoa needs twenty souls to race. When the schedule is set for six months or so, Bruce Kendall sends an information circular to his mailing list, asking for interest and commitment by return mail. Based on the response, Bruce and Jim assess the talent available and make a race-by-race selection. That no more than fifty are on the list reflects the positive and sustained response over the years. There are a dozen crewmen who have been all over the world with *Kialoa* and had the time of their lives, even playing by the house rules: pay your own plane fare to wherever the boat is located; no women allowed to sleep on board; put the toilet lid down after using so that towels won't fall in; keep clean sheets on your bunk, and make it up when you aren't in it; keep your gear and yourself clean. Speak your piece, then follow orders. The Collective.

The Fantasy, for many who are struck as mere children with the terminal disease called sailing, always involves a dream boat of majestic proportions that plies the oceans of the world, making a hundred mysterious landfalls, each more enchanting than the last, with its crew sampling the world's people, cultures, foods, wines, and women. Fraternizing, perhaps, with the rich and powerful, and in the best possible way.

Kilroy has made all that a reality, and a palatable one by doing it Right. He has taken this crew along, and done it with perfect management. The test of that is how few *Kialoa* crewmen think, in their hearts, that they could do it any better.

A good percentage of the crew on any Super Boat these days will be New Zealanders, or "Kiwis," as they are called after their national bird. Kiwis go ocean racing like Austrians ski – naturally, enthusiastically, and with great ability and grace. As a group, they seem lean and strong, ruggedly handsome, and likable. They are patently laid back, stoically self-reliant, confoundingly taciturn, disarmingly wry when they do say something, and hustlers of a proficiency that makes one glad to be a mark. In general, they seem a strange lot. The strangeness comes from a fierce love and loyalty for their homeland that has collided with an even fiercer pragmatism that says they will have to leave New Zealand in order to make a buck. So they typically hitch a ride on the first worthy yacht that has a place open, and off they go for two, four, ten years to see the world, and maybe make a good deal for themselves. As Bruce Kendall has.

Bruce Kendall met Jim Kilroy in 1969 during Cowes Week. He was then twenty-two. By that age he was not only familiar with farming (sheep, cattle), having grown up on a ranch, and sailing (his father, like nearly everyone in New Zealand, had a boat), but he was also a qualified marine engineer, having served a five-year apprenticeship as part of his schooling. Self-reliant. Kilroy needed a skipper at that point, and Kendall was it. Most skippers are big on maintenance, small on racing. Not Kendall. He has been captain of the opposite watch virtually since he stepped on board. And he has redefined dedication by his unwillingness to put anything before the boat – including, one year, a Christmas present for his wife.

But it has paid off. The ride he hitched out of New Zealand wasn't much, but he came home seven years later for the Tasman Sea Race as captain of the Big Dream. In the small, sail-crazy confines of New Zealand, he was an instant national hero. Fifty boat-loads of well-wishers greeted *Kialoa* as she entered the harbor. Horns and whistles. Kendall and *Kialoa*. Television interviews. Not a bar on the island would take his money. Not a woman on the island wasn't tinged with lust.

In 1978 Kendall retired as skipper of *Kialoa* and became an employee of Kilroy Industries. Assistant to the president. In charge of boats. He started at the top. An office. A secretary. A title on the door. It was inevitable. If two people can work easily together on something as complex and fraught with ego pressures as fortunes of an ocean racer, they can work easily on any problem. So when Kendall isn't doing boat work, Jim will ask him to take a look at this problem or that, do a little trouble shooting, and report directly to him. Assistant to the president. Kendall is like a second son to Kilroy. His salary is generous. He is well on his way to becoming a millionaire. As head of the *Kialoa* Industrial Complex, he's got terrific indus-trial connections. He's got a new house in Seal Beach.

A new BMW in the garage. A beautiful wife. He is still watch captain on the boat, number two to Kilroy, which isn't bad. And he knows, in his heart, if only on account of the numbers of sailing miles and years that are behind him – Bruce loves his H-P too – that he is the better sailor.

He is also the proof for star-struck New Zealand boys that the whole amazing trip is possible. The proof, and often the Connection. He is in charge of their dream. The Kendall/*Kialoa* Connection. There were nine Kiwis on *Kialoa* for Cowes Week and the Fastnet Race. Selected by Kendall. Good guys. Good sailors. Taciturn. Self-reliant. Wry. Strange.

The rest of *Kialoa*'s crew is spread out across the United States, coast to coast, from the Canadian border to the Gulf of Mexico. They are from many walks of life and a wide range of financial means. Kilroy has had to lend many of them the plane fare to make various races. They have always paid him back. But whether their lodgings are meager quarters in low-rent districts or more lavish digs, they all have one thing in common: the pictures. They all have the T-shirts too, but those are buried in drawers. The pictures are a prominent part of every crewman's home décor. They have to be, they are so large, matted and framed behind glass. Kilroy issues them from time to time, like stock dividends. There have been eight or ten different ones over the years. There is an aerial view of *Kialoa* in midocean running before forty knots of breeze with about a million square feet of sail billowing; a water-level shot of the boat on the wind; a long-distance aerial of it against a Tasmanian headland—all gorgeous photographs, reproduced in high-quality color prints.

Like stock dividends, they serve a purpose. They promote the Fantasy, reinforce the Big Dream, cement the *Kialoa* Family. It is Kilroy's way of sharing, his way of keeping the wonderful hook of the Dream deeply set. The pictures are important.

There are no superstars among this crew. All of them found themselves on the boat in the course of sailing events, and set about learning what to do with the monster under the cool hand of Jim and the more "mad Prussian" approach of Bruce Kendall. They got aboard, and they liked it. More than that, the compatibility factor was high. They really liked sailing with each other, meeting in various exotic ports of the world to sail the Big Dream, and then live it ashore with dinners and parties, wine and women. The Family took shape. They practiced hard and when it didn't work they talked about it and practiced more. Every race was a reunion of high spirits, good racing, good times. They got wild, they got drunk, they carried on, and they began to have a winner on their hands. And as long as they remembered the rules – no women sleeping on board; keep the toilet lid down so the towels won't fall in; clean sheets; bunk made up; keep clean; speak your piece and follow orders – Jim was happy. *Kialoa* was happy.

And given that all owners are nuts, Jim was OK. The unilateral decisions were his (and Kendall's), but they knew he was hanging it out there with them. Jim set limits for them, but they took his measure too, and helped define the limits. Like the time he wanted to wipe down all the boat's flatware with alcohol. On one long race some sort of flu bug had been brought on board. Jim was casting heavy looks at the alleged culprit. Then he began thinking. Germs. Germs on board, on my boat. What to do, what kills germs? Alcohol kills germs. Get out the alcohol and wipe down the flatware was the answer. No one really minded if Jim was hooked on keeping his feet sterile with the regular application of antiseptic solutions and powders. He was the owner, after all, and all owners are nuts. Just be thankful he doesn't like cigars. But wipe down the flatware with alcohol? It was suggested that all the flatware and plenty of alcohol would be brought to his cabin if he really wanted that job done.

Jim was cool. He knew when to back off. He is fond of saying that he doesn't want any zombies on board, that he wants people who think. And that is what he's got. Thinkers, some first-rate talkers, a few very fast-lipped humorists, all of them thick as thieves. They are the best Directed Collective a man could want assembled on one deck. Their loyalty is unfailing, and so is Jim's. Stuart Williamson, a biology teacher from Belmont, California, who has been sailing with Kilroy for ten years, was in charge of trimming the mizzen (the sail on the after mast) on the ketch. *Kialoa* is now a sloop. Williamson's mast is gone, but not his job. Williamson is somewhat puzzled by this turn of events. An old-timer among the crew, he belittles himself as a length of old hemp that has tried, with only moderate success, to turn into Dacron as the technology has accelerated. But he admits that once "in" with Kilroy, a fellow would have to do something truly dastardly to be bounced. There is still plenty for Williamson to do, mast or no mast. He's good. But when in doubt, he slides below and does the dishes. (He's that good.)

Over the last few years Kilroy has taken the Family concept another step by bringing some of the *Kialoa* crew into his business. He has watched out for them, kept tabs on their fortunes, and if things have looked bleak for them, or they have run out of good ideas, he talks business. Four *Kialoa* regulars are now full-time employees of Kilroy Industries, which means they spend a lot less time sailing and a lot more time making money. But it seems an acceptable transition all around.

It is a strange marriage, this mixture of school-teachers, businessmen, salesmen, engineers, displaced Kiwi professionals, and Jim Kilroy. But it seems to work. Sensitivity is high, especially so from Kilroy. He knows his limitations, knows when to keep a low profile, like after parties when the serious drinking and jiving starts. Kilroy is an awkward social animal. Subjects like seismic loading go over like lead balloons in casual groups. And he is not a drinker. The party is not his favorite milieu. Fingers could definitely relate to that, and to the way Kilroy purposefully wandered off one evening at Cowes to be by himself, to walk several miles around the island and then find a quiet spot to have a solitary bite of dinner. But even when he does get caught in the wrong place, Kilroy can usually blast out of it. Like the night before the Fastnet Race, after the party he gave in the house he had rented for himself and the crew.

It was late, and Kilroy returned to the house and wandered into the kitchen where an elbow-to-elbow crowd of stalwarts were well into serious drinking and jiving, having discovered a half bottle of vodka that had to be finished because everybody was leaving the next day and you can't lug along a half bottle of vodka on the Fastnet Race, even if Jim does permit the occasional alcohol ration at sunset to take the chill off. So it had to be finished. Drink up. Wash it down with beer. The noise level in the kitchen was extraordinary. The first-rate talkers and fast-lipped humorists of the group were in excellent form. The funny lines were overlapping and the laughter was physically exhausting. Good times, an integral part of the Big Dream. It was Cowes Week, after all, and the party had been a good one. The steaks had been tough as hell, the booze was fifteen dollars a bottle, the ice ran out, and the night had been too damn cold for the patio, but it all simply meant that this was bloody England, the Isle of Wight, and here everybody was, together again, with the Fastnet Race tomorrow and then back on the damn plane, back to the old grind, so this was it for sailing and racing, drinking and jiving, have another.

Jim walked into the middle of this late-night kitchen madness, into the midst of these fine lads and their ladies, his extended *Kialoa* Family, those who share the Big Dream with him, and they greeted the keeper of their Fantasy with a cheer of appropriate spontaneity and window-rattling volume that brought the color rushing to his face from the very bottoms of his sterilized feet.

And then one of the fast-lipped humorists grabbed the floor and put together a rather long, complex, vodka-inspired, and amazingly articulate toast that was humorous mainly at Jim's expense, concluding with the demand for a speech from Jim in which he was charged to tell this overstimulated gathering of drinkers and jivers why and how *Kialoa* was going to win the Fastnet Race, in ten words or less please.

Jim hesitated only a moment. His eyes darted up to the flat surfaces of the kitchen cabinets where he found what he was searching for, and he looked back at the toast maker and said with a smile, simply, "luck." One word for ten. A 90-percent saving. A triumph! The place went wild with people beating appreciation on the counters with the flat of their hands and cheering. The howls of approval followed Jim down the hallway and must have echoed in his head long after he shut his door and went to bed. The stuff of sweet dreams.

Fifteen people died and four yachts were lost during the race.

TWO

The ferocity of the storm began to take its toll even on *Kialoa*. Radio reports had indicated all kinds of trouble developing behind us, and occasionally word would be passed to the deck from Christie Steinman, the navigator, about the increasing number of boats, planes, and helicopters responding to distress calls. No one thought seriously about turning around to help. We were probably a hundred miles ahead (south) of the yachts that needed help most. Even at twelve knots it would be eight hours before we could arrive on their scene.

"Probably" is the key word. Boats in an ocean race rarely know the positions of more than a half-dozen competitors, and those are usually boats of their own size and speed. It is difficult to imagine how three hundred and three sailboats that all start within an hour of one another and that are all going to the same place can so quickly lose track of one another. But they do. With perfect visibility a boat is hull down at fifteen miles. The ocean seems to obliterate competitors at a distance. Electronics solves the problem. The boats with those passenger-jet navigation areas know exactly where they are and where they want to go and why, and how the stock market closed as well. And radio communication is excellent. But boats in ocean races don't keep their radios on simply because they don't want to talk to each other. Loose talk afloat is for Sunday power boaters and commercial fishermen. Sailors don't fraternize on the radio. For sailors, fraternizing on the radio is like being loud at a golf match, intoxicated in public. For all their technological warfare and systemized big-business approach, most people who go ocean racing really like being at sea. They like it for old-fashioned reasons: communing with nature, getting away from the hustle and bustle of land, breathing the best-smelling air in the world, showing a little courage in a primal form. They don't want the damn phones ringing. Had they wanted to talk with anybody who isn't on the boat, they would have invited them along. Nor do they want to give away their positions. They are racing.

In some races radio talk among boats is illegal. Certainly it was against the rules for boats on Admiral's Cup teams to compare notes during races. If not, it would have been a battle of radios, not boats. And in the Fastnet Race, the British decided to shut down all those passenger-jet navigation areas in the interest of fairness to the less-well-equipped boats. For people who enjoy lukewarm beer, who wash their hair bent double in bathtubs, and who have made "sorry" into their national word, it was consistent thinking. Radio direction finders were allowed, a concession of dubious worth. RDFs have a reputation just slightly above life rafts in terms of effectiveness. On aluminum boats they don't work at all. Recording depth finders were allowed. Fortunately.

Most boats were proceeding around the course by dead reckoning (DR), a time-honored system by which one keeps periodic records of the compass course steered, boat speed, wind speed and direction, sea state, current set, the altitude of passing birds, and whatever else might seem helpful, all modified by a critical seat-of-the-pants factor. Based on these data, little x's are penciled on the chart and then connected like numbers in a children's puzzle. Instead of a moose in the woods, what materializes is history: the course the boat has followed up to its present position. More or less. Using DR is like playing piano. If you don't practice, you get rusty. Navigators used to the electronic game are not good dead reckoners. Theoretically, star and sun sights can be taken with the sextant for more accurate navigation. But this was the British Isles, where the sun shines only when it is not on duty in southern California, leaving the skies cloudy many a day.

Christie sat below for six or seven hours during the storm watching the depth recorder. By comparing its ups and downs with water depths shown on the chart, she could tell more or less when we passed over two big underwater banks on the way to Bishop Rock, our southern turning mark. More or less. Our distance to the west of Bishop Rock was very imprecise. Like *Kialoa*, a lot of boats had only a vague idea of their positions. By the time boats in trouble went for their loran sets, the instruments might have been broken or shorted out. When it was time to give the rescue service a position, it was very vague indeed. Too vague.

We knew only vaguely where we were, and even more vaguely where boats in trouble were. And we were starting to get very busy ourselves. At first, we sat on deck encouraging the helmsman when he made a particularly adroit move to avoid a wave that looked certain to nail us. Driving was exhausting. The helmsman needed encouragement. He faced painfully into blowing scud that stung like sand, looking for the optimum path through confused seas that lifted us up and up, and either rolled under us or struck us full force. The helmsman would yell a warning the moment he knew he had been beaten by one of the monsters. We would double our grip and tuck our heads in as thousands of gallons of solid water tried to batter us off the deck. We listened to gear straining, watched it work as the loads increased, felt the awesome forces tearing at the boat in a dozen directions at once from the sudden braking action of her bow slugging into a wave, or from waves falling on us broadside at the same time that heavy gusts struck. It didn't seem possible that gear and vessel could bear such loads in combination with the terrible shocks they were receiving. One had to marvel at *Kialoa*'s performance, and also hope it was not short-lived.

The outhaul was the first to go. This was a piece of three-quarter-inch braided Dacron line rigged through a sheave at the end of the boom to the number-three reef cringle of the shortened sail. Its job was to stretch the foot of the sail taut along the boom. It had been chafing in the sheave, out of sight of our constant inspection for chafe, and it parted with the sound of a rifle shot.

The crew was so attuned to the possibility of gear failure that we all jumped at once, like sprinters coming off the blocks. Speed is of the essence when gear fails because the failure usually places an overload on other gear, with a potential domino effect. In this case, the reef cringle was also tied around the boom to hold it down, but now the mainsail had inched forward along the boom in puckers, putting great strain on small reef lines that went through lightly reinforced grommet holes in the sail itself. The whole middle of the sail could have been torn apart. Four men did a quick job reaving a new line and taking tension. They would get better at it. That outhaul would part twice more before the night was over.

As the positions got shuffled around on the rail, Fingers found himself sitting next to the running backstay wires. Two multistrand stainless wires were attached to the mast at heights of forty and sixty-six feet. They were joined together about eight feet off the deck by a metal plate from which a block was hung. Another wire of equal strength dead-ended on the deck, passed up through the block, ran back to the deck through another block, and aft to a large winch. This was the running backstay, whose job was to support the middle of the huge mast, keep it from collapsing forward from the strain of headsails, especially staysails, which do not hoist to the masthead. And it was a small staysail that was helping pull *Kialoa* through the night at twelve knots.

As reluctant as he was to move, since any movement was accomplished with great effort and discomfort, Fingers moved. There are certain unwritten rules of behavior that one has to believe in. Like really making sure that the oven has been turned off before leaving the house. Like getting up in the night to check an anchor line at the slightest suspicion of slippage. Like staying outside the "V" ("the slingshot") formed by a line or cable under tension. Like keeping one's distance from any heavily tensioned member of the rig unless performing a specific job. Bruce Kendall was very nearly killed a few years before when one of *Kialoa*'s big spinnaker guy wires snapped. The boat was racing in smooth water in Block Island Sound and took a big knockdown with the spinnaker set. Bruce was on the weather rail trying to organize the disaster party when the guy parted. Quick reflexes and some luck saved his life. He ducked, and the recoiling wire lashed him across the top of the head instead of the forehead or temple. It took eighty stitches to close him up. He had to wear a baseball batting helmet on the boat for two years. He still has a bump on his scalp that itches when someone asks him about it.

Fingers grabbed the running backstay wire and tested it. It was under big tension. He moved. Ten minutes later the block hanging from the metal plate exploded.

Several of the crew scrambled. The staysail was quickly lowered to take forward pressure off the mast. The main was trimmed to bring pressure aft. The deck lights came on. The mast was wobbling like it might have been made of plastic or hard rubber. It was a frightening sight to see the one thousand-seventy-three-pound, ninety-five-foot column of extruded, welded aluminum so out of control. Disaster seemed imminent. It felt like an awful loss of balance at a critical moment -- catching an edge while streaking down a mountain on skis, or stubbing a toe while crossing hurriedly against a flashing "don't walk" sign in bad traffic. There didn't seem to be any way the mast could take such a whipping for very long without coming down.

From the number of eyes darting glances aloft, it was a general expectation. For a moment after the failure, there was disorientation. There was so much wind and sea noise to cut through. It was difficult to see. Then we knew it was the runner. But where had it broken? Aloft, in the mast? On deck? Was it the wire? The wire was tested for twelve thousand five hundred pounds, the block for twenty-eight thousand. We were lucky it was the block, which turned out to have suffered a crystallized weldment. If it had been the wire to the mast, it would have taken hours to repair. And someone would have had to ascend that wobbly stick to do it. But one of the crew quickly scrambled to leeward and retrieved the metal plate, which was swinging around wildly. We got a line from the deck to the plate for temporary relief to the spar. It was done with one eye for the job and one eye for the mast. If the mast did fall there was no predicting which direction it would go. The thought made the back of Fingers' neck prickle.

By the time a new block was attached to the plate and the wire reassembled, an hour had passed. But the mast was still standing. That was an immense credit to Hood Yacht Systems, that had engineered and built it. But the boat was being sailed gingerly during that period. We spent an hour at half speed. Because it was thought the mast might have sustained serious damage, the staysail was not raised again. Without it, we were two knots slower.

But our priorities had shifted quite properly from racing to win, to racing to finish. Down one notch. It would cost us.

With the boat back on course and the crisis settled for the moment, we once again clipped onto the weather rail and huddled together, each of us privately assessing his personal discomfort, measuring energy reserves, checking endurance levels, and wondering how much worse it would get before it got better.

Fingers took a look around him and really observed the night for the first time. Since he stepped on deck his attention had been buried in one job or another. He had seen the storm only peripherally. Now with time on his hands he focused on it and wondered if it was a dream.

Unlike the claustrophobic, ominous feel of most storms, this one presented the striking contrast of clear skies alight with a full complement of stars. Occasional clusters of low, fast-moving fleecy clouds would pass through. The moon was high, three-quarters full, and brilliant, illuminating the steep seas with cold, eerie light. When clouds masked it, its beams peeked through to dapple small patches of ocean with pure pounded silver. Astern, the Big Dipper was full to brimming.

It roared a special kind of beauty, this night. Beauty of the sort that cuts deep, leaves marks. Fingers had always relied upon the sea to restore him, and the sea had never let him down. He lived by it, fished and dreamed upon it, planned and schemed beside it. It nurtured him like a great mother. For him its beauty would never be surpassed. He knew that. But this night something shook him besides the howling gusts and their driven volleys of water that pressed his soaked inner garments against his chilled skin. Fingers sensed something. He was not a churchgoer, but at sea his agnosticism always faltered. At sea was when the concept of cosmic unity was most difficult to deny. This night it was impossible. Fingers felt out there, connected, wide open, hitched for a moment to a bit of business that is the stuff of man's greatest fantasy. Awed, Fingers concentrated, engraving silver-blue images on his brain.

Kialoa was reaching at ten knots under reefed main only. Her fine racing bow sliced into the seas, carving off hunks of ocean that were splattered to either side as foam, and heaved high into the air and blown into the sails. The water was thick with globs of phosphorescence that would stick on the sail and glow for a moment, or speed off to leeward on the wind like sparks from spent fireworks. From her mad dash through the storm, *Kialoa* was leaving a swath of pure white foam astern fully two hundred yards long that shimmered like a snowfield in the moonlight. Fingers yearned to watch *Kialoa* pass from a nearby vantage point. We must be a sight, he thought.

In the glow of the red deck lights crewmen moved to and fro, glistening wet in their bulky white foul-weather suits, moving awkwardly in slow motion, like space travelers caught in a hostile, top-sy-turvy environment. Faces, even bodies, were indistinguishable. Names that some had written on their jackets in marking pencil were fragile reminders of life on earth.

Fingers was fatigued, cold. It had been better with work to do. Now there was nothing to do but sit on the hard, nonskid aluminum deck and endure, a necessary and essentially thankless task, complicated by discomfort and a nagging desire to use a recrimination or two. Endurance was such a head game.

He thought a lot about turning the corner, arriving at Bishop Rock on the southwest tip of the treacherous Scilly Islands, leaving it to port, then easing the sheets and heading downwind back to England. Turning the corner. It had a nice ring to it. But how long would it be? Three hours? Four? Six? The storm had hit *Kialoa* about seventy-five miles northwest of the Bishop. How long had it been since then? Fingers had lost track of time. He would try to get a position, talk to Christie. It would help to know how long one had to bang his head against the wall. Because thinking about turning the corner would pull him through; turning the corner (ahh), running off, rum and Cokes, soothing tokes.

To pass the time he began a serious search for Bishop Rock. Serious, but impossible. Visibility was good, if one could focus properly between clouds of wind-driven spray, and if the boat was on top of a wave at those moments and not down in the trough putting a thirty-foot wall between him and the Bishop. The Bishop wasn't helping with its stingy two white flashes every fifteen seconds. Maybe the Scilly Islanders had extinguished the light, or hung lanterns from the necks of meandering cows, as they once did to lure cargo-laden sailing ships to their doom during storms. The islanders would murder the survivors, then loot the vessels. But he continued to search with diligence. What else was there to do? Better an impossible task at hand than rerunning old Clint Eastwood movies, or dwelling on the problems with his woman (the fifteen-year hitch), or other troublesome alternatives that were lying in ambush. So he searched, and thought about his small herd of sheep and his cats and dogs, about taking piano lessons again and laying in wood for winter, about his woman (in spite of himself) and playing pool at Duffy's Putnam County roadhouse. Occasionally a passage from a familiar piece of music would pass through his head, providing a welcome sound track. Wagner and Beethoven were best for this night.

Nothing really distracted him from the extraordinary hardness of the cold deck, or the discomfort of the water that sneaked through gaps in his foul-weather armor and trickled against his skin. He made himself take deep breaths, and from time to time he flapped his elbows vigorously like an aroused penguin. He checked, and realized he was functioning. He looked around, and found that several of his fellows were lapsing into a head-down body slump that announced they were temporarily taking their leave, entering mental hibernation, checking out, sorry about that . . . they weren't responding to the various calls to attention for this little job or that. Fingers seized upon this forfeited energy, picked it up and swallowed it like Popeye devours spinach, and with the same empowering result. It wasn't a trait he was especially proud of, energy leeching. So be it. Since he had come on board, he had been laying back, playing new boy on a new boat, taking it slow, doing a set of dinner dishes (for twenty!) because he believed new boys should do that sort of thing. But now he began running around in his customary fashion, hell this was a boat like any other, just a big bastard, responding to jobs three people away from him.

When there was help needed aft to dig the storm sails out of the bottom of a cockpit locker, he was there. When the bulky number-five jib was ordered forward, he grabbed the huge, heavy thing and struggled forward with it, dragging and rolling it along the slanting deck like a huge beanbag chair filled with lead shot. Halfway forward he slipped, and he and the sail slid down the deck until his safety harness went taut. Cursing, he struggled to his knees. A large body loomed over him. It was Alastair, one of the Kiwis. Alastair reached down and grabbed the bag by the neck and picked it up. "No short cuts, mate," Alastair said, and moved forward with the burden.

Stuart Williamson was thinking about his garden. He was estimating six more hours to the corner, and the thought seriously dismayed him. He was cold. He worked to displace his mind, and it ended up in his garden. When I get home, he thought, I will garden. And he thought about old sticks and dirt and compost being fed into the shredder, watching happily as the shredder spewed out a soft pile of fine organic material that the seedlings would treasure. It was better than thinking about what would happen if the mast broke.

Stuart was a flier, and he was comparing flying in bad weather with his current discomfort. Lurching and bumping through the air versus this. About the same. A wing could fall off, the engine could stall, but then the mast could go too. Better chance of survival on the ocean, probably, but until the wing fell off flying was warmer, and drier. If only he could stay as warm and dry as he was at home he would like ocean racing a lot better. Stuart counted the positive aspects, and was glad this weather hadn't hit at the start of the Transatlantic Race that he had recently completed on *Kialoa*. That would have meant nine days to go. Nine days! The worst. For sure the mast would have gone, and he might never have gotten warm again.

Stuart allowed himself to dwell on a favorite puzzle: Why he went ocean racing time after time. Why anybody did. Why he had been a regular on *Kialoa* for ten years. Why he had spent all that money on plane tickets, all those weeks beating his head against the bulkhead and freezing his ass when he could have been touring Spain (Olé!) or planting shallots. He had never been in a sport where more people who swore they would never go again kept showing up. Take the Sydney-Hobart Race. Now there was a monster outing. Long, cold, and always an unpleasant surprise, a storm, dead calm, and always totally unpredictable and unexpected until it was right on top of you. Sydney-Hobart. It had a nice ring to it. A trip to Australia. He could understand why people did it once. But twice, three times, six times? Jesus. Was it masochism?

Maybe it was latent heroism. When Stuart got home people said they had prayed for him. People he hadn't heard from in years wrote him admiring letters. Stuart was astounded. "I would have had to burn my house down with me in it to get that kind of response," Stuart said.

There was no sport quite like it, Stuart knew that. No one waved the yellow flag if there was a wreck and oil got on the track, or if it began to rain. You started and you kept going. Dates for races were set months (years) in advance, weather be damned. One could count the ocean race cancellations over the years on half the fingers of one hand. He knew that the idea of living through it was important; there was something about the sea and man.

Walking through Cowes, the night before the start of the race, we had passed a pink-and-white tent from which music emanated. A handwritten sign nailed to a post announced "film 7 p.m." It was just after the appointed hour, so we squeezed into the tent in time to see the film Qantas Airlines produced about the 1977 Sydney-Hobart Race. They had picked a good year for filming. A bad storm struck the fleet, disabling dozens of boats. A hero helicopter pilot had flown a dauntless cameraman close by the mast tips of floundering yachts, and some of the resulting footage was spectacular. The film also captured the very moment a one-hundred-eighty-degree wind shift struck *Kialoa* at twenty-five knots, showing her heads-up reaction as she doused sails and regrouped and was back on course in less than twenty minutes. She went on to win.

"During that film was the only time I've had a strong insight into why I do it," Stuart said. "There was one shot that got to me. It was after the storm had passed and *Kialoa* was sailing about three miles off this huge vertical headland in about twenty knots of breeze, looking beautiful and white against a smoothly textured sea and the dark cliffs. Then the camera zoomed back and we got smaller and smaller, less and less significant as true perspective was gained, and it took my breath away—I said, 'that's me! I'm there!' "

A still photograph of *Kialoa* against that Tasmanian headland hangs in Stuart's house in California. It is by far his favorite because it best fulfills his fantasy, expresses the freedom of the Dream: "It has something to do with the infiniteness of water, its vastness; it doesn't inhibit vision."

The Dream again. To compare the Dream to the reality, one condenses the reality into the photograph for more favorable measurement. The mysterious chill of a real landfall (the return from limbo) is underpainted for maximum romantic satisfaction in the literature of the sea: *Moby-Dick*, *Two Years Before the Mast*, *Captains Courageous*, *The Nigger of the Narcissus*. There is heavy romance in those pages, of course, but after a while one has to admit how out-weighed it is by the pain and suffering, the cracked and bleeding hands and the scurvy, the madness and cruelty, the plank walking and keel hauling, the flogging and fighting. Listen to poet John Masefield, from "A Ballad of John Silver":

> *Then the dead men fouled the scuppers and*
> *the wounded filled the chains,*
> *and the paint-work all was spatter-dashed*
> *with other people's brains.*
> *She was boarded, she was looted, she was*
> *scutled till she sank,*
> *And the pale survivors left us by the medium*
> *of the plank*

Or this from Masefield, from "Evening—Regatta Day":

> *Your nose is a red jelly, your mouth's a tooth-*
> *less wreck. And I'm atop of you, banging your*
> *head upon the dirty deck;*
> *And both your eyes are bunged and blind like*
> *those of a mewling pup,*
> *For you're the juggins who caught the crab*
> *and lost the ship the Cup*

Or perhaps that is the grim stuff of romance—the sharing, by one's very presence on the ocean in a situation of stressful threshold exploration, of all that pain and suffering, of all the blood that has run in all the scuppers, of hanging it out (primal courage) in the name of that ancient and ghastly and heroic and undeniably seductive tradition of the sea and man.

There is the occasional shot of pure bliss, too. What Stuart calls "the total body charge" one receives when everything is perfect, when all is right with the world. "The guns!" Stuart says, exulting "the guns!" closing his eyes the better to hear them again, the better to hear the highly-polished brass cannons whose lovely voices are reserved for the first three boats that cross the finish line, throaty voices that never fail to rattle the stomach and stop the heart for at least one beat.

"In 1971 we did the Tasman Sea Race," Stuart says. "We were first to finish, first on corrected time, and set a new course record. The whole race was sailed in perfect weather. We never needed foul-weather gear. To make the finish line at the end we had to execute a jibe in heavy going. It was perfect. The chute never so much as trembled. When the gun went off it brought tears to our eyes. Twenty cases of beer were waiting for us at the dock."

But ocean racing mimics life. Pure bliss is a great rarity. The pictures help sustain it, of course, help make it possible to come to terms with the stranger need for one's fair share of abuse.

Fingers was still chuckling to himself over Alastair's remark. At least this wasn't boring. There had been enough boring moments over the previous winter and summer with sailors and sailing to last him a while. Kicking and screaming he had gone down to

Antigua to cover Race Week for one of the yachting magazines. The sun did a number on his winterized New England skin. He got too drunk on the rum, too stoned on the dope. Wasting away again. The racing was good on one of the smaller boats, the water an ethereal color, the island high-sided and smooth with green vegetation. But mainly it was a zoo of sexless, bare-breasted women and boring men, many with the cocaine blues, all expressing an unpleasant aura of aggressive detachment. Their only real sin was their lifelessness. Everybody drank heavily. The men talked exclusively about jib round, keel sweep angles, end-plate effects, fractional rigs. Worse than golfers. The women more or less covered their breasts at night and did their Robinson Crusoe best to look suntan torrid and Caribbean wanton. But their eyes betrayed their confusion, their lack of real interest. With all the exposed, jiggling flesh it was hard to believe, but swinging Antigua Race Week felt like the most difficult place in the world to get laid. Fingers got the unmistakable sense that nothing was happening. Meanwhile, back home, people were slugging it out in gasoline lines.

The stuff he wrote was so hostile and negative that the genteel boating magazine editors, whose job after all is printing the pictures and reinforcing the Fantasy, shook their heads and made throaty sounds of discontent.

Fingers blamed some of it on his own attitude, which wasn't good. His bummers ran in two-and-a-half-year cycles, and he was smack in the middle of one at that point, a winter of discontent. As usual, at such times, he was spending many hours reviewing lists of alternative occupations and lifestyles, to no avail, although short-order cook continued to interest him. This particular cycle was complicated by the fifteen-year hitch, which is like the seven-year itch times two and then some. So few couples make it through fifteen years in one piece that there is very little research available on the subject. After fifteen years, one enters a void. Just when you think you know someone, the surprises flood in like bugs through a hole in the screen door. Suddenly it is all strange and puzzling and different and confusing, unless of course one can recall how it was the last time he was forty.

Fingers had brought his woman to Antigua, and even that injection of paradise -- contemplation on warm sand -- had fallen short. When she left prematurely he went over to the afternoon beach-party madness to take pictures. A kid climbing a coconut palm dislodged one of the heavy, football-sized fruits. It fell on Fingers' face and upraised camera. His nose bled copiously, but it wasn't broken, and the event did provide a grand opportunity to wash down a little yellow pain-killer with several rum and Cokes and lie back and ponder just what it could all mean.

Then there had been Block Island Week, an annual summer festival off the New England coast, with many of the same boats, names, and faces. Block Island Week was held together by a little firmer cement in the persons of several old salts, robust gentlemen of years who sailed and raced for the pure love of it, and in the same spirit that men once climbed for half a day to make one run down a favorite ski trail, long before lifts were built. But the parties, the boozing, the bands, even the sailing seemed awfully repetitious.

When the Fastnet Race came up, Fingers had misgivings about going. He found it hard to generate enthusiasm for the trip. Sailing was a beautiful pastime. The only problem was that it usually had to be done with other people. That was one reason he sailed Sunfish. Ocean racing meant a lot of other people, many of them strangers, usually, and in very close quarters. On *Kialoa*, it meant nineteen other people, all of them strangers. It meant another ocean race with its company of men far removed from the enigmatic world of women. It meant stepping into a page out of Joseph Conrad's masculine world wherein willpower would be tested in the face of natural forces, where concepts like initiation and spiritual transformation went hand in hand with courage, and loyalty to the outlaw brotherhood. The hearts of sailors worth their salt were supposed to be stirred by such swashbuckling expectations. But the anticipation of another four-day stint in the confines of a strange vessel among men he didn't know was failing to get Fingers psyched. Sometimes he wondered if he hadn't had all the romance he could stand. And from experience he knew that the fraternity of the outlaw brotherhood, the company of men, simply wasn't all it was cracked up to be.

Fingers had sailed many a pleasant mile with just his woman. Together they had put in some good miles with one other carefully selected couple. That was the way to go, he thought. Close friends and the sea. He liked having women on boats. After the sea, they couldn't be beat. Together the two were a great combination. Women lent a touch of civility to tight shipboard quarters. And love and the sea, sex and the sea, those weren't bad combinations either. But in light of the current female state of mind, generally, Conrad's company of men was looking more attractive than it used to. Women were certainly having problems, and those problems were often making their companionship a chore.

The ordeal of their "liberation," for want of a better label, was taking its toll. Now it was women who had stopped to examine themselves. Fingers knew it was possible to still have fun with the occasional woman, but the encounter had surely lost some of its luster. Too many women these days seemed bent on proving something to themselves, and were seizing upon various men as targets of opportunity. Or it was couched in the form of a tacit challenge that wasn't very sexy.

Fingers knew it was a tough transitional period for women. And because there were so many of them, and men can't really live without them, and they were so fantastic, every bit of them – all that delightful plumage designed to attract, and their crafty, cunning, often brilliant minds, so different from men's -- that it was also a tough time for men. A joyless time. Men were hurting.

Men were partially to blame. But not totally. Fingers wouldn't buy the extremist point of view. But he knew men had exerted their wills, tailored their lives around themselves, lived where they wanted to live, made a lot of unilateral decisions, and generally put the women in prisons with a few kids to take care of while they went to the office or the golf course or ocean racing or wherever. Then eighteen years later, if it lasted that long, the kids who had been propping the ladies up took off for college or jobs, and there was a second and more serious case of postpartum blues. When that got straightened out, along came menopause.

Indeed, woman's scene had been grim. Something had to be done, and it was in progress. Fingers loved seeing women on construction sites. A year ago he had worked in a boatyard beside a woman who was good at carpentry, great on varnish, and attractive as hell. What a combination. Recently he had met a woman at a party who was welding submarine hulls. Why not? And he admired *Kialoa*'s navigator, Christie Steinman. Christie had grown up out West riding quarter horses. She learned to sail at her mother's insistence when the family moved to California. She went to college in Hawaii where she fell amongst boat bums, and learned to navigate while bringing boats back to the mainland from Honolulu. She was good, very low key, and smart enough to be nervous about the responsibility of taking seventy-nine feet of Maxi Boat with a crew of eighteen men around the Fastnet course in good weather, let alone in one of the more vicious storms in memory. And attractive as hell. What a combination. She was also sensible enough to realize there were a number of things that were important to her before marriage and kids and all the rest. She was trying out as the first female navigator on a twelve-meter, and doing a fine job from all reports, and enjoying it.

But basically, Fingers looked forward to the third or fourth stage of all this liberation, the stage when women began to feel it was OK to like men again, OK to trust them, OK to play with them, OK to act sexy, and OK to get it on. Life was too damn short as it was.

Fingers actually didn't have much choice about going on the Fastnet. The assignment he had accepted was *Kialoa*, world ocean racer, and it would be necessary to see her in action somewhere in the world other than Florida or Newport, Rhode Island. So he bit the bullet and took off once again into the company of men.

It had gotten so he dreaded the travel part. His arms always went numb when he slept on airplanes. He got jet lag from crossing even one time zone. At London's Heathrow Airport he rented a car and near-missed his way to Southampton, struggling with right-hand drive, left-hand shifting, keeping left unless passing, and the terrible urge to fall asleep. Somehow, in the random tangle of Southampton streets, he found the rental agency and pulled in, shaking visibly from one of the more frightening rides of his life.

Things began to brighten up as he boarded the hydrofoil for the high-speed ride across the Solent to Cowes. It had been blowing forty knots all day.

With its wicked currents and famous short, steep chop, the Solent was a mess. But the tough little hydrofoil soared across in great time, unperturbed by the weather.

The first glimpse of Cowes was striking. Cowes Week has a reputation for great numbers of boats all enjoying great sailing, and in fact an astounding number of boats were jammed into the harbor. Even in forty knots of breeze the fast current was turning moored boats stern to the chop, bouncing them mercilessly. Hydrofoils and Hovercrafts buzzed and zipped around, manned by trim chaps in smart blue uniforms with braid who looked like colonels at least. The yacht club with its crusty stone wall to the sea and its impressive row of brass cannons looked as if it had grown out of the hillside. The enormous sliding doors of the Hovercraft hanger were painted with a Union Jack that was at least seventy-five by one hundred and fifty feet in size. It put an unmistakable stamp on the proceedings.

The streets of Cowes were overflowing. Every shop, every pub, every restaurant and fish-and-chips stand, every grocery, liquor, nautical supply store, and novelty shop was crammed with people. People didn't walk, they flowed along the narrow, winding cobblestone streets of the quaint town. And all of them were yachtsmen. Fingers struggled along heavily burdened with his bag of sailing gear, feeling his arms getting longer and trying to get some bearings on the *Kialoa* house, trying to pretend he wasn't seeing the same faces once again. It was like going to rock concerts or making political street scenes in the 1960s. The same kind of homogeneity prevailed. The same acid heads would be carrying signs, beating drums, and selling drugs. The same overweight earthy lady would be nursing her kid while screaming foul epithets. The same people would get arrested. The same gang would have on the freakiest costumes. After a while everything looked the same. Special interest must breed physical resemblance. Or maybe clothes do make the person, as Thomas Watson insisted at IBM. What Watson really understood was that people want to look the same. There is satisfaction in numbers, security in likeness.

Take any bunch of advocates, like sailors, dress them all in blue or orange boots, faded jeans, alligator shirts with boat names embroidered over the left breast, bulky sweaters and down jackets, toss a yellow foul-weather jacket over the ensemble and you have a recognizable mass—a bloody army.

It was difficult for Fingers not to be disparaging. Familiarity does breed contempt. Too many of them were red-pants, madras-jacket creeps who learned to sail as brats at some fancy yacht club near their parents' (or grandparents') summer home. After Harvard or Stanford, Amherst, Williams, or some experimental school since folded, they went to work in the family company, or used their share of the family money to dabble in real estate or natural-gas exploration, or perhaps to buy gold. And since sailing was as much an Old Family Tradition as their tweed sport jackets from J. Press, off they went as often as possible, muttering tag lines from beer commercials, hi ho. As an army they often made Fingers feel like an Italian trying to make it in Switzerland.

Tradition was the key word. Some of them were damn good sailors who could hang it out with the best Kiwis. And they got in shape by jogging or playing squash and racquet ball. Maybe they stopped smoking, and occasionally they got divorces. But most of their lives happened in a safe zone, in the circle of Wall Street and private clubs, over the strong safety net of financial security, under the misapprehension that there was a Right Thing and they were doing it. They willingly drove fifty-five miles per hour, convinced it was a law one could live with. Most of the time their idea of "going for it" meant another cold beer from the fridge during a TV time-out. Risk, for this group, had always been a prefabricated, well-calculated entity.

Fingers regularly read editor Lewis Lapham's "Easy Chair" columns in *Harper's*. Lapham, he thought, had as keen a grasp on the hell-bent culture as anyone. He kept a clip from one of Lapham's columns taped to his refrigerator: "The national obsession with health (cf. the princely sums spent on jogging and diets as well as in the hospitals and research laboratories) reflects the refined sensibility of people grown too delicate for the world." When he read that over he had thought about the familiar faces he had been seeing over the past year in Antigua, Block Island, now Cowes; over the past ten years everywhere. He thought there was truth in it. He thought it applied. What really horrified him was the nagging possibility that it might apply to himself as well.

A new group of familiar faces had been added to the mix of yachtsmen in recent years. These belonged to a swarm of professional sailors: designers, builders, rigging specialists, consultants, marine hardware representatives, and mostly, sailmakers. Like arms merchants, their job was to get out there and harvest dissatisfaction. And it was so simple. Take, for example, a discouraged owner who was getting whipped regularly. Maybe it was the sails. So he would call the sailmaker, and the following weekend he would have not just a sailmaker, but a star on board his boat, a young fellow who was a least a former collegiate All-American, national class champion, or maybe even an Olympian. And this dashing young guy would be full of talent and charm and information, and he would look at the existing sails and refrain from saying straight out that they were terrible, but the owner would catch a few carefully dropped facial expressions, and the guy would let himself sound excited about what his loft's exclusive shape concept could do for a boat like this one, not to mention the improved holding characteristics of their newly developed fabric weaving and coating techniques. And the owner would think, maybe there is hope for this old bucket after all.

Then the young star would come back in a few weeks with the new sails in hand, and damned if the old bucket didn't finish in the top five! Zowie! Of course it had been somewhat of a help that the star had maneuvered the boat at the start, and steered most of the weather leg, and dictated the downwind tactics, and trimmed the chute. But the taste of victory was too sweet. Quickly the professionalism could accelerate. It would depend on how much of his soul the owner wanted to apportion to the young star (and the star's hotshot friends); how much the owner could give up and still rightly feel it was his boat, his trophies that were accumulating on the shelf. Some owners said the hell with it, and simply underwrote the project and organized a factory team of sailmakers, designers, builders, and free-lance hotshots to race the boat.

As a business selling technique, the on-board professional approach was legitimate, and that kind of aggressiveness was one of the factors that had moved the sedate (but rigorous) sport of ocean racing through such a quantum leap into an era of high-tech threshold exploration. But the changes the professionals had wrought in the sport were not all good. Racing against these guys was often like Columbia playing the Pittsburgh Steelers. Fingers recognized the professionals in the crowded streets of Cowes. It was easy to pick them out. They were perpetually tanned and red-eyed from a steady diet of sun and salt. He knew many of them, and some were friends. But this day they all looked like insurance men packing heart-attack machines.

At the *Kialoa* house Fingers began the often awkward integration process of becoming a part of this tight-knit fraternity—this company of men—of becoming a crew member, of sharing, for a while, the Fantasy. It wasn't too hard. They were accepting people, friendlier than a lot of crews he had been with. There was plenty to do. The crew party was that evening and it wasn't being catered. This was the comprehensive *Kialoa* crew. They raced the boat, delivered it, fixed it, and gave their own parties. The *Kialoa* Industrial and Culinary Complex. There were problems to be solved: how many heads of lettuce were required to make a salad for thirty people? Estimates ranged from three to ten. Jim and Bruce were both gone, and they had their H-Ps with them. This problem would have to be solved in the head.

The party was a success. Four heads of lettuce sufficed. The fireworks display afterwards at the harbor was the most spectacular Fingers had ever seen. A great crowd lined every inch of the Cowes waterfront as the aerial rockets drenched the slick, now-placid waters with an array of brilliant colors, and strobe-lit more than a thousand sailboats trying to rest for the following day's excitement. The booms and cracks were immense. The next evening was when Fingers stumbled upon the 1977 Sydney-Hobart Race film and saw *Kialoa* doing her thing. Things were looking up. Excitement was building. Little did he know that the upcoming storm would make the filmed report look tame by comparison.

The start of the Fastnet Race was extraordinary for its confusion of yachts. In addition to the Fastnet, several inshore races for smaller boats were getting underway. The Solent seemed bank to bank with boats. The race committee started the smaller

Fastnet classes first, until only the Maxis and other class A boats were left jockeying for the line with all the brass and assertiveness of dinghies. Bruce was calling the starting tactics in a voice whose higher pitch and increased volume attested to his excitement. Jim was at the helm concentrating on keeping the boat moving smoothly and listening to Bruce. The two worked well together. Jim maneuvered his Big Dream in close quarters. We tacked, we jibed, we ran the line, we listened to Christie counting down the seconds, we marveled at the nearness of the surging boats to the right and left of us all converging as the final seconds ticked off—"nineteen, eighteen, seventeen,"—the tense faces in the cockpits glaring their determination to hold their rightful courses (watch out!); fifty-, sixty-, seventy-, eighty-footers all at full power, the distance between them measured in arm lengths, hitting the line at speed within a few seconds of the gun, a fantastic sight, a feat to be compared with blind Zen archery—sailing's contribution to great moments in sport.

The excitement sustained as we chased the smaller boats west out of the Solent, making frequent tacks inshore to avoid the onrushing current. We dueled *Condor*, who had been hard on our heels at the start, as we began carefully picking our way through the crosstown traffic of boats we were overtaking. Naturally we caught a great gaggle of them as the Solent closed to its most narrow point. Somehow, everyone squeezed through the thousand-yard cut. Even though *Kialoa* stole their wind, or caused them to divert, the crews on the smaller race boats were more enthralled than upset by her intrusion. Their water-level view of the Big Dream passing was worth the moment's loss of speed. Some of their crewmen rushed below for cameras.

In the light air the fleet stayed bunched until evening. It was the last we would see of all but a few boats. With the dawn we would be sailing alone, in front of the fleet. We would miss the grim excitement at a little bight of land called Portland Bill where a dozen or two yachts were imprisoned that first night by a vicious little eddy that wouldn't let them go. They doused their sails (some of them) and waited as long as four hours for tide to change or the air to freshen. But there was at least joy in the numbers. One could watch a competitor's running lights moving rapidly astern as he was seized by the current, and find humor in one's adversary's plight if not one's own. Because the next time around the crazy eddy at Portland Bill it would be him sliding astern as the laughter echoed across the water. It was maddening, it was crazy, but it was fun.

It was the essential stuff of Cowes Week, Admiral's Cup, the Fastnet Race, the feature that makes this meeting such a favored one among the racing sailors of the world. For the tidal currents along the English shore of the Channel—in concert with the tricky winds that funnel through—have no equal for deviousness. To manipulate them to one's advantage is a notion that has captivated sailors' imaginations since man first spread canvas aloft to catch the wind.

More than four hundred years ago—just fifty miles west of Portland Bill, along the Fastnet Race course—the great seaman and pirate Francis Drake was using his local knowledge of the current to outfox the approaching ships of the fearsome Spanish Armada. For Drake it was life and death, not a silver trophy, that was at stake. George Malcom Thomson describes the situation in his lively book, *Sir Francis Drake.*

"Drake, with eight ships, probably took an independent course. As a Plymouth man, he knew that, while with an ebbing tide a current set up-channel, there was a back-current which set westwards toward Rame Head. Six hours would suffice to bring the ships round the promontory; another six hours and the inshore current would take them west of Looe."

Kialoa had to struggle with the currents, but she did so alone. Boats like *Kialoa* share their fortunes with no one. They surge to the front and stay there. In fifty races over the last four years *Kialoa* had been first to finish forty times. (Ah, the guns!)

On *Kialoa* the routine set in. We slept three hours, we stood watch three hours, with longer shifts during the day. The tasks quickly became repetitious. We trimmed an inch or so, we eased it back, and did it again and again. We flopped the sheet and made up our bunks for the people on watch. We kept the toilet-seat cover down so the towels wouldn't fall in. We spoke our pieces and followed orders. We sat long hours on the deck as *Kialoa* slipped through the gray chill of the Irish Sea. We ate too much at meals. We suffered ennui.

"Time," Stuart Williamson said, "never passes so slowly as it has when I have been sailing. It's awful. You sit and watch the sail for hours. My God, it is boring. It is ten times worse than cricket. Or it is uncomfortable, tilted, hard to walk. You have to sit sideways in the john. Or if it's rough you stagger around in your duck suit."

On Sunday evening Jim put on a tape of Richard Harris singing some of his poetry. We ate steak and vegetables and potatoes and bread as we sailed on the Irish Sea. It felt like a theme party. It was at such times that Stuart liked to think about the lobster boat he wanted to buy. Now that was the way to have a good time. Motor along the coast. Stop here and there. None of this sailing crap.

On Monday around noon, someone roused Fingers from his dreamless sleep and told him if he wanted to see Fastnet Rock, now was his chance. He extricated himself from his second-story bunk and stuck his head up the companionway. It was dramatic, this rock. The jagged top of some steep, underwater pinnacle, it rose one hundred feet, straight up. Until it was lighted, it must have been some awful hazard. Someone tapped his leg. He was blocking the hatch. He went back to bed.

A few hours later Jim said he thought we had a shot at the record.

The storm had certainly changed the complexion of things. Time wasn't dragging now. With Fastnet Rock seventy miles astern and all hell breaking loose in mid-ocean, it was anything but boring. Ennui had departed for warmer, drier places. Fingers felt fit. His adrenalin was pumping. He struggled about the deck clipped on and doing jobs or just sitting for long periods, taking deep breaths and flapping his arms to get warm, contemplating the amazing spectacle howling and heaving on all sides of him, the huge breaking moonlit seas, the streaking trails of phosphorescence, the stars and fleecy clouds, etching the mad scene with acid in his mind while a tune from The Band kept haunting him, an old tune, a sweet song from yesterday:

> *Wonder could you ever know me*
> *know the reason why I live*
> *is there nothing you can show me*
> *life seems so little to give?"*

Because this was it. This was freaking it.

Bad ears and a complex of allergies took Fingers from the pollen-ridden interior of Massachusetts to the Tabor Academy Summer Program on Cape Cod when he was nine. There, with great reluctance, he learned to swim. He learned to swim for the simple reason that the program had a rule: no swim, no sail. And even at a distance, sailboats had been sucking him in. He had a transponder in his brain that was tuned to the sound they made, to the flapping of sails and the rattling of bronze clips on sail tracks, to the sensuous gurgle of water on hulls; to the froth of bow waves and the burble of wakes. Not to mention the sights. And so this Cancer, who was later assured by a well-known 1960s astrology hustler who listed herself in the Manhattan directory as Birdfeather Barbara, that his chart was full of water, got his feet wet.

He could remember to this day his tentative, frightened descent of the ladder at the dock the afternoon of the swim test. When the water level rose to the pit of his stomach, his heart began to strangle in his chest. The blood backed up and roared in his temples, impairing vision. His knuckles were white on the ladder rungs. His legs threatened to collapse. He shuddered at the look of the befouled anchor chain to the dock that disappeared into the depths like a slimy, linked serpent. He tried to speak but he could not. The instructor, a wise old man, a hairy, barrel-chested fireplug named Kelly out of the New Bedford, Massachusetts, YMCA, two of whose seven children had become variously a nun and a priest, told him in his gravelly voice to climb back out. From that moment he understood salvation.

Somehow, painfully, he learned to swim. And at the hands of a quiet, gracious figure of a man named Francis Tower, who arrived at the dock each morning in freshly laundered khakis with a heavy ditty bag of his own construction bending the right shoulder of his spare frame, he learned to sail. Because Francis Tower thought such things were important, he also learned to read charts, splice and whip line, tie knots blindfolded and behind his back, sew canvas, scull a skiff with one oar, sail backwards and without using the helm, and make dock landings so perfect that imaginary eggs placed between the dock and the bow of the boat would be touched, but not damaged. At the start of the first race he ever skippered, he learned the importance of wearing shorts. The excitement was such that his bladder released and he soaked a pair of stiff new dungarees that chafed him raw before the race was through.

On Sunday evenings, vespers were held in the main building, a grand, low-ceilinged Tudor room hung with large oil paintings of former headmasters and benefactors. One hundred and fifty chairs were arranged in a semicircle facing the huge fireplace and its flanking diamond-pane, leaded windows that looked southwest across the harbor. One hundred and fifty boys aged nine to fifteen would reflect the glow of the setting sun with their white sailor suits—the Sunday uniform—as the speaker mused about man and God and law. The younger boys fidgeted. The older boys sat raptly concentrating on the tasty young counsellors' wives who were always in attendance.

Vespers closed with a group singing of the hymn, "Now the Day Is Over." Fingers had sung the hymn for five summers as a camper, two as a counsellor, eight times each summer, and it never failed to move him. Especially the third verse:

> *Grant to little children*
> *Visions bright of Thee;*
> *Guard the sailors tossing*
> *On the deep, blue sea.*

The sailors tossing on the deep blue sea! It was an early image, set as with chisels in stone. One only had to look around at the sailor suits—behold oneself—to begin the romantic vision. Wasn't he sitting there wearing a sailor suit? It wasn't a real one, but a sailor suit none the less. Then wasn't this a hymn about him and the rest of the campers, those baby-faced kids sitting all around him with the Brylcreemed hair, some of them with impetigo splotches gaily painted with Gentian Violet? Christ, the romance of it was too much. Beyond the diamond-pane windows a harbor full of sailboats pulled gently at their moorings in the sunset. Coupled with all those swollen-breasted counsellors' wives with their suckling babes in arms—a vision to make any boy's sailor pants begin to take a strain—it became indelible. Religion and romance and lust make a package that is difficult to beat.

He knew he was a terminal case when he gave up a hard-won position on the baseball team to accept a coveted invitation to take a four-day cruise to Maine on a seventy-foot yawl the Academy had received as a gift. The walk to the coach's house had been his longest to that point. He learned that making a decision was a lot easier than carrying it out. Even if he was a stumbling third baseman whose inability to hit Junior Cape League pitching was compounded by his difficulty with the long throw to first. Coach Moose Reilly, who stood six-foot-six and who had once been a serious first-base candidate for the Boston Red Sox, was dismayed and just a touch threatened, but understanding. Fingers somehow held himself together during the negotiations which terminated his contract (he had to terminate—the big game would be played during the cruise), but he shuffled all the way back to his dormitory spilling tears.

The cruise to Maine was far beyond his fondest expectations. The yacht was fifteen or twenty-years-old, and in perfect condition, one of Olin Stephens' exemplary designs. Unlike today's yachts, it was made of nothing but the friendliest of materials: mahogany, cedar, fir, spruce, teak, and brass, with real canvas sails and lines of linen and cotton. It felt like a yacht should feel, smelled of paint and varnish, pine tar and caulking, canvas and old coffee, like a yacht should smell, and it creaked a little under sail, just to let everyone know it was making an earnest effort. It was painted white, the proper color for a yacht. Its name, *Tabor Boy*, on the stern was in gold leaf.

One balmy, clear night on the cruise they kept sailing as promised. When it was Fingers' turn off watch he climbed into the upper bunk he had drawn and lay there, experiencing for the first time the gentle sleep-inducing motion of a large sailing vessel. When he turned over, half asleep, he bumped against the overhead. Fingers suddenly felt very claustrophobic, perhaps because he had been reading, at the time, Edgar Allan Poe's tales of premature burial, in which luckless souls with rare diseases that caused them to appear dead were mistakenly interred. His thirteen-year-old imagination resisted logic. So he got up, and dressed, and by this turn of events learned the pleasures of a night sail under the stars, of the cozy companionship of the cockpit with its quiet, intermittent conversation, the faces tinged with a red glow from the binnacle light, the black water seeming to slip past the hull twice as fast as the instruments would indicate. After that night, that cruise, he was truly beyond hope.

At the end of that summer the closing exercises held more wonders in store. There were awards for the tennis ladder, and the summer racing series in the various classes, and for excellence in wood shop and riflery, baseball and archery. And then a surprise. The director began reading a citation for overall excellence, and he went on with Fingers only half listening because he was brooding a bit about not winning the tennis trophy, and suddenly there was great cheering and clapping, and the white sailor suits on all sides were shoving at him (was this a joke?) and whacking him on the back, and he realized with astonishment that it had been him the director had been talking about. He had won something big. Best Camper. At age thirteen. The best! Even as he stumbled forward, propelled by the applause, the strangeness of the concept occurred to him. "The best"?

In later years what would strike him most was the purity of that award. He hadn't competed for it. It had just happened. They gave the award for only two summers, then had to discontinue it. It seems that it encouraged goal-oriented behavior (more commonly known as brown-nosing); gave rise to the tactics and the scheming and the games that winning always engenders. He learned about that, too. He learned about that in college when he mounted a campaign to snake his freshman roommate's girl friend, to win her in the time-honored American Dream tradition of magazine fiction and made-for-TV movie plots. Because his tactics and scheming and games were well-conceived, he succeeded. He got the girl. He got his trophy. Having won, what was left but to get married? It took only a short time to realize the full extent of his folly. Bob Dylan rubbed it in with a riddle. "There's no success like failure," sang that inscrutable harmonica player from Hibbing, "and failure's no success at all." What was left but to get divorced?

Since then he had been careful about winning, careful to curb his competitive urge over matters more significant than killer Frisbee, volleyball, tennis, sailing races, and Osage-orange bowling. His competitive nature was strong and healthy, but he let it out gingerly and prudently. He knew from experience that in this Number-One crazed society that was still hysterically grinding away under the impression that winning was the only thing (in words usually attributed to a late football coach who was widely thought to also have been great), winning could definitely get in the way of living.

Boats kept getting in the way too. The summer after his first year of college, Fingers landed a job as first mate on a twelve-meter. The boat kept a busy racing schedule, even though she was a heavy old wood-hulled boat with pine decks and wooden spars.

But the mahogany joiner work below was a joy to behold. The winches were cast brass that could be turned to silver with dedicated polishing. She was a far cry from the efficient modern twelves, but a gold-plated flier just the same. His deal was a hundred twenty-five dollars a week plus khaki uniforms, a bunk in the forecastle, and all he could eat. That wasn't bad for 1957.

His boss was Captain John Corson, a thirty-year-old, blue-eyed devil with black curly locks that fell onto a sullen face handsome enough to win him the nickname "Hollywood." Whenever Fingers thought of that summer, the shoes stuck in his mind. One of the first things Hollywood John mentioned to Fingers as he was adjusting to the routine of sanding, varnishing, and polishing was the shoes. Whenever he came on board at night he was to be on the lookout for a pair of ladies' shoes on deck by the boarding ladder. The shoes would let him know that three would be a crowd in the forecastle that night, and he should seek accommodations either aft or, even better, ashore. It turned out to be the summer of the shoes. Fingers became familiar with a great variety of shoe styles and heel heights, especially when the boat was in Oyster Bay, New York, its home port. Even when it was hauled out for bottom work. That so many women would be willing to climb a rickety ten-foot ladder to the deck in high heels to enjoy Hollywood's affections was as fine a tribute as a man could want. Enviable. Fingers swore that the occasional back pain he later suffered could be traced to the many nights he spent cramped up in the back of his 1941 Ford sedan.

That summer was when he learned to treasure the comradeship of the hard-core professional boat crews. Unlike many of today's skippers who are college dropouts or hustlers looking to parlay a boat job into a piece of the owner's company, these were old-timers (even at thirty), loners, outcasts of a sort who were stoically committed to life before the mast; whose pride rested in the mirror quality of a varnished cap rail, in the glow of a freshly bronze-wooled and bleached teak deck. Almost to a man, they were professional drinkers as well.

Among the younger skippers and mates, a day off started at 10 a.m. with shots and beers at one of Oyster Bay's black bars, where the rum tasted like prom perfume and the jukebox never let you down. By early afternoon, a pleasant state of euphoric semi-consciousness had been reached, a period during which it was possible for people to perform the most amazing feats of destruction upon automobiles, driving them in such a way as to render them totally unrecognizable, and then, more amazing, returning to the bar on foot with only a few streaks of blood clotting on their foreheads to tell the stories over another drink.

Hollywood lost his treasured gull-gray Caddy convertible with the red leather seats that way. It happened so close to the bar where he was drinking that he heard the crash. The guy who had borrowed the car had been unable to navigate for more than a hundred yards. But he was a great mate of Hollywood's, and it was an hysterical sight when the guy and the girl he was making off with came staggering in, the girl in tears of fright, and it was a terrific story that would keep getting better. Hollywood saved the steering wheel and the baby booties that hung from the mirror, and things would even out, he knew that. Things always did.

Usually on Friday night, Hollywood, his mate who had wrecked the Caddy, and Fingers would drive ninety minutes into Manhattan for some serious excitement they were certain awaited them around Times Square. Hollywood always drove in. It was his concession to fairness. Fingers would be left to attempt the drive home, at 4 a.m., which he always managed for fear that if he faltered, Hollywood's mate would end up at the wheel of the treasured Ford. After the first Friday venture into the city, it had taken the three half-crippled sailors as systematic a two-hour search of the midtown, West Side streets as they could muster to locate the elusive car. After that, Fingers began writing the numbers of the cross streets where they parked on a piece of paper that he would put in his left shirt pocket. It was a habit that never left him.

A few Fridays later they got their serious excitement. The guy on Broadway who offered them exotic women sounded sincere, even though the cab ride to 125th Street did take forever. When the guy demanded a down payment in advance, even that seemed reasonable to three determined drunks in the wee hours of the morning. When he said he didn't take out-of-town checks, they could understand that too.

A guy could get burned with a check. It was only the moment they saw the guy's back rapidly disappearing up the stairs of the creepy apartment building with their money that they realized they had been fleeced. "Murphied," in the jargon of the mean streets. That night's drive home seemed longer than usual, if that was possible.

The Friday nights made the Saturday mornings difficult. Saturday was race day, the day the strap-hangers from the city showed up full of huff and puff, lawyers and advertising executives, stockbrokers and financiers, all anxious to vent spleenloads of vileness that had accumulated during another hectic week of commuting and martini lunches and near misses. There were always one or two visiting yachtsmen who loved to bug Hollywood or Fingers about flag protocol, remind them about the precision with which good boat crews raised and lowered such critical pennants as "owner absent, guests aboard" (a blue square with a diagonal white stripe). These people were the ones who faded noticeably, turning a strange pale-green color when the going got rough. There was some satisfaction to be gained by dropping a very wet coil of heavy line on their heads, or by scuffing a boot against white knuckles that were death-gripped around a winch. Inadvertently of course, and with profuse apologies.

But the sailing was great. The racing was memorable, and even the cruising wasn't so bad, including the two weeks the boat spent in Martha's Vineyard when life got so consummately boring that Fingers and Hollywood broke the rule about keeping one man on the boat at all times, and began going ashore together and drinking themselves into oblivion, often riding borrowed bicycles off the dock into the harbor.

At the end of that summer there was a moment when returning to college seemed like absolutely the wrong thing to do. The life was great, and with all the fringe benefits and a hundred twenty-five dollars a week besides, it was a tough decision. But Fingers went back to college. Three years later, after graduation, his first "substantial" job would pay him a hundred dollars a week. And at that he had to buy his own suits.

At one hundred dollars a week, even with annual raises, it took a while to accumulate enough money for a boat. But Fingers finally found a spare three hundred dollars with which he purchased an eighteen-foot Bahamian-type sloop from a boatyard out on the tip of Long Island. Fingers would learn, eventually, that he was too hung up on boats, too susceptible to any line resembling a fair curve to be trusted with the purchase of one. When it came to looking at boats with even the vaguest notion of buying, he stopped working right, like a sugar-freak kid in a candy store with a few cents in his clenched fist. Looking at boats he would begin to feel light in the head, sweaty of brow, and whatever powers of logic and reason he possessed would depart with the confused fluttering of startled geese.

The Bahamian boat, which he named *Conch*, was old. It had not been in the water for three seasons.

He had seen window shutters that were tighter than Conch's planking. But the boatyard guy affirmed that she was cedar and would swell up tight as a drum after a week or two on the bottom of the creek. Who could assail such salty logic? Who could ignore the conspiratorial rise of an eyebrow reserved for fellow mariners? At his most devious, a man with a boat to sell can make horse traders and car salesmen look like humanitarians.

Like the predators they are, men with boats to sell can spot a weakened quarry at a distance, and they take fiendish pleasure toying with them like cats with crippled mice. This guy graciously threw in an old twelve-foot rowing boat that any self-respecting group of geraniums would have spurned. With oars and locks. That clinched the deal.

A few weeks later, after Conch had been pulled out of the creek and seemed to be floating, Fingers and a friend of his who had assured him that he had once "commanded men at sea" while a junior officer in the navy, set sail from the tip of Long Island with the object of bringing Conch down the Sound to Larchmont, to moor her off the Larchmont Yacht Club, of which Fingers had just become a member. They stowed extra gear and food in the "dinghy," and therein hung a kerosene lantern from a makeshift mast for atmosphere, and in the interest of safety.

Fingers' friend clutched the tiller with authority and tenacity for most of the trip across the Sound while Fingers pumped every thirty minutes... or less. It was fortunate he had remembered the pump. The former navy officer kept the helm all day until late afternoon when the breeze piped up and came aft, riling up the Sound and causing the shallow-draft Conch to roll gleefully in wide arcs. Then and only then did the navy officer leave the helm so he could hold on with both hands and vomit with abandon.

The one-hundred-mile trip to Larchmont was made in three widely-spaced weekend jaunts, and must have created a spectacle on the Sound that wouldn't soon be forgotten by the more proper yachtsmen who passed by with binoculars staringly fixed. Best of all was the rainy Sunday when Conch arrived in Larchmont after a long, wet sail, with oranges and less compact foodstuffs (a thoroughly wet carton of eggs, butter, and cold meat in greasy cellophane bags) sloshing in the kerosene and seawater mixture in the bilges of both the mother ship and her dinghy. The lantern hung blackened and rusty on the makeshift mast. There was, about Conch's overall presence and the condition of its crew, the look of those who might have just arrived from England on the dubious end of a frightful bet. With his woman handling the sheets, Fingers smartly shot a mooring directly in front of the big windows of the stately, tradition-bound club, behind which many fashionably attired members were posturing over Sunday supper.

They cleaned up the big pieces, furled the sails, retrieved the foghorn from the bilge, emptied it of water, and blew three mighty gargled toots to attract the attention of one of the club's immaculate, turn-of-the-century launches. It was a moment that made the whole trip worthwhile.

Two years later, after the third impatient note came from the club inquiring about the disposition of the Bahamian sloop that was drying out behind one of the storage barns, Fingers slipped the dock-master ten dollars to burn it the next time he was cleaning up.

Though many years would pass between the eighteen-foot Bahamian sloop and the purchase of a second boat, it would take even longer for Fingers to catch a glimmer of enlightenment about the great difficulty of transforming one's adoration of boats into their ownership.

His dream of a boat of his own was a very old and repetitious one. Over the years the dream had attained mythical proportions: If only there was a good-sized sailboat that afforded periodic escape into the ocean, life could be almost perfect. And so when some money came down out of the blue, it had "boat" written all over it. After a search, there it was, a classic little wooden yawl, dark green with a gold-leaf cove stripe and a small bowsprit, lying peacefully at her mooring in one of those seemingly landlocked Maine coves, in profile against a rough horizon of pines. Idyllic. Love at first sight. Sweaty of brow.

There was a purchase and sales agreement, a thorough survey, and the myth was reduced to oak, mahogany, spruce, brass, lead, and Dacron. He painted it gray and renamed it *Smoke*. Three weeks after hitching it to a mooring in the harbor near his home, after a two-day sail from Maine during which he accumulated a discouraging four-page list of changes and alterations the boat needed, a hurricane came up the coast and hit the harbor with heavy winds. *Smoke* was properly secured, but the forty-footer next door broke loose and clawed *Smoke* before proceeding out of the harbor to its own destruction. The damage was measured in four figures. It was covered by insurance, but it was a portentous beginning.

As the summer passed it became evident that there was time either to work on maintaining the boat (paint, varnish, etc.), or to sail it, but not enough for both. Or money. Many a sunny day Fingers would glance up from varnishing and look wistfully at all the sails on the horizon. He began to feel woefully self-enslaved. Then the storm in the Himalayas struck, and by the time he had picked up the pieces it was December, and freezing cold, and *Smoke* was secure in wet storage but not covered. The day the cover went on he found himself chopping four inches of ice out of the teak and varnished mahogany cockpit with an icepick. He was mortified. *Smoke* was sold the next year, an event which only added complexity to the question of whether the happiest day of one's life was buying a boat or selling it.

There were certain things Fingers understood about *Smoke*. It had been a premature move. He had been overreaching financially. And it had been a frantic effort at stabilization that was wishful thinking at best. The notion that one might eventually attain a state of being in a specific place that satisfied some abstract and compound imaginary vision—a situation wherein enjoying life could really begin—one that it would be possible to sustain (stop the world) was a fallacy that had raised havoc in the culture. It was a misguided, old-fashioned myth that had been subtly and tenaciously ingrained in people since elementary school. Fingers had known people whose lives really appeared to have reached such a level. They were people whose hair was always in place, whose habits were unalterable, whose good cheer was inevitable, whose cars never had a mess inside and always start-ed, whose nails and screws were lined up by size in glass jars in their workshops, whose garages were al-ways well swept. They had responsible jobs that paid well. They served on alumni committees. They moved to the summer house on the same weekend each year. They had arrived at a designated place—a state of being—and were enjoying life.

Fingers hadn't really believed in it. But the con-cept was ingrained. He kept being fooled. *Smoke* had fooled him. But he didn't hold a grudge. He had known better.

Every so often there was truth in advertising. It was such a truth that first tipped him off some years ago. "Getting there," read a slogan coined for the Cu-nard Line, "is half the fun." Then he had paid a visit to a little monastery in upstate New York. A "skete," it was called; a group of eleven monks gathered around a twelfth who functioned as a father figure. This particular group were disenchanted Franciscans who had split with the church to pursue a religious life of their own design. By day they raised sheep and calves for their commercial slaughterhouse, and German shepherd dogs. By night they prayed and discussed weighty issues among themselves. In response to Fingers' clumsy inquiries about what lay ahead for them, they patiently explained their belief that the only meaningful goals were immediate ones, that each day, each hour, each minute, was an end in itself. They explained that the "there" in "getting there" was pure myth. No such place existed. Getting there wasn't half the fun, it was all the fun. The trip itself was the goal.

The morning after that discussion, Fingers had stood with one of the monks watching a magnificently horned Dorset ram making the rounds of thirty or so ewes in his efforts to assure a bounty of spring lambs. The animals were confined in a paddock inside a barn that was dramatically lit by shafts of dusty sunlight. It was quiet. The herd was passive, relaxed. The animals' breathing and chewing were the dominant sounds. Their collective backs formed an immense blanket of soft wool that undulated here and there when they moved. The place smelled like wool, felt like wool. The posts and boards of the paddock had been polished to a glowing patina by the animals' natural oils. He had never watched a ram at work before. He and the monk stayed in the cozy barn for at least thirty minutes observing the ram's gentle exploratory nudges at one ewe's shoulder with his forefoot, his slow move astern, the humorous curl of his upper lip that registered his approval of the aromas present, and then his efforts at mounting the ewe. Sometimes the ewe would walk away. Sometimes she would stand. The ram was placid throughout. All in a day's work.

The monk was a pleasant, raw-boned kid in his twenties. In his jeans and mackinaw he looked like any farm boy. He enjoyed the ram's game as much as Fingers, had just as many smiles going. Fingers kept wanting to ask the monk if watching the ram didn't make him miss a certain part of life. The monk was young, healthy, smart, handsome. Did becoming a monk eliminate natural urges? The question formed itself a dozen times, but was never asked.

Fingers kept in touch with the monks long enough to learn that his shepherd friend contracted pneumonia that winter and died suddenly. It made him wish he had asked. But perhaps it was as well that he hadn't. Questions weren't necessary to assess that monk's joy of life, nor to understand that his joy wasn't founded in anticipation. The skete's focus on the trip, not the destination, smacked of truth. It didn't seem possible that those men of God, and twelve million members of Alcoholics Anonymous ("one day at a time") could be wrong.

Condor, *first to finish and course record setter in 1979 Fastnet Race.*

THREE

Fingers was washed overboard about 2 a.m. He had been one of the work party that had been trying to bring the excess cloth of the mainsail under control. When the reef had been tied in, the great mass of lazy sail had been gathered and lashed upon the boom. Gust after gust had worked at the packet's leading edge until the whole thing had blown out and formed a large inflated tube to leeward. Six men were braced against the boom, taking the weather on their backs, and not making much progress trying to reduce the size of the billowing tube. Someone broke out lengths of half-inch line, thinking that if the lines could be threaded through the lightly reinforced grommets in the sail it would be like attaching reins to a runaway horse. There would at least be something to haul on.

The lines were threaded by one man kneeling on the boom as another held him, while the vessel bucked and reared. But now the ends were streaming down to leeward, under the sail. Fingers dropped to his knees and went under the boom. With one hand on the lifeline for support, he reached up and grabbed one of the whipping, elusive lines just as *Kialoa* smacked into a large sea. He felt the onrushing wall of water before he saw it. Even as he looked forward, he knew it would be there, tearing down the deck faster than surf on a beach, giving him no time to react. He was right. As he looked and registered that the entire lee deck of the boat was underwater, it hit him. He was swept off his feet into the torrent, streaming like a plug on a trolling line.

A few years ago the door of a passenger jet cruising at thirty thousand feet blew off. A stewardess standing nearby was sucked out into the night. *The New Yorker* published a fine poem about it. The poet pictured the woman's descent as one in which she was gradually divested of her garments by the slipstream, until she plunged to the earth as naked as she had been born. Fingers had always wondered what her last vision had been like. The poet hadn't gone into that.

His last vision would have been a great one. He would have surfaced in the middle of that glittering snowfield astern, with the foam hissing all around him like the head on warm Coke poured over ice. And there would be *Kialoa* streaking away into the night, rising and falling on the seas; a night so clear he would have been able to see the boat plainly for a thousand yards. But he didn't think about that at the time.

At the time he thought about the same old discomfort of water up the nose, water stinging his spray-battered eyes and blocking his ears. And as he felt the safety harness tighten on his chest as it took the load, he pictured its working end wrapped around the hydraulic boom vang cylinder and clipped back on itself. He thought about the clip of the harness, pictured its sturdy design shape, and recalled how tough the spring-loaded part had been on chilled fingers. He thought about the webbing, the stitches. He thought about Steve Lirakis, who had made the belt, handing him a promotional T-shirt the last time he had seen him on Thames Street in Newport a year ago. He thought kindly of Lirakis bent over his sewing machine—Lirakis, who was now in charge of his life.

His right hand, he realized, had closed over the lifeline and was stabilizing him nicely. When the heavy water drained away and the lee side finally lifted, he swung himself over the lifeline to the deck. By his safety line he hauled himself to higher ground and slumped half-sitting, half-kneeling on the deck, as out of breath as if he had just finished a brisk, twenty-minute run. He was soaked through. That made sense. He had been swimming. His boots were still with him, amazingly enough, but full. His heart was pounding well above the aerobic rate suggested for a person of his age and weight, rapping out a pulse that was deafening. Hackneyed exclamatory words kept running through his mind like an old pot-party tape loop. The whole event hadn't taken more than fifteen seconds. It hadn't even really been a close call, but it had certainly been more of a thrill than he had bargained for. The word "rush," co-opted in the 1960s by drug users to describe the effect of high-quality goods, had just been given new meaning. The force of water that hit him was astonishing. He had gone over like a chip of wood. The feeling of total helplessness was immensely sobering. Then why was he chuckling to himself? Nervousness? Relief? One fact dawned on him as he slumped on the deck, gathering his wits, and it gave him pause: in the darkness and confusion of wind, water, and noise, no one had seen him go over. If something had failed—the belt, the cylinder—he wouldn't have been missed until it was too late.

He went back to the job at hand, hoping to stave off the chill of being soaked by working. Keep moving. He went back to his position at the boom, alongside the guy he had been working with. It was suddenly important to share his anxious moment with someone, bring it to sharper reality by the telling.

"I just went over the side," he yelled through the wind.

"No shit?" the guy said, looking his way. "Are you OK?"

"Yeah."

"That's good," the guy said. And they went back to work.

At the cocktail party he attended after he got home, Fingers began unwittingly to antagonize people by telling them, when they asked, that he hadn't been scared during the race. Much to his surprise people challenged him, wouldn't believe it, or they would join an adjacent group of cocktail talkers from which they could conveniently cast hostile glances his way. And he hadn't even mentioned going over the side. Not to that bunch. The men were in high-tone brightly colored slacks, some imprinted with turtles, and blazers with golf- and yacht-club patches sewn on the breast pockets. Their shirts were daring plaids, their neckties natty. The ladies were in pink and green, with cable-stitch cardigans draped over the shoulders against the evening chill, their little embroidered handbags adorned with whales and sea birds, their designer eyeglasses perched atop their heads. They were up in the rental house for a month, up from the Connecticut suburbs, Park Avenue Manhattan, Main Line Philadelphia. Their kids were taking tennis lessons at the club and smoking dope (snorting coke) behind the seventh green while mom and dad dried out on the beach between cocktail parties. The Summer People. No, they were not the ones to tell about going over the side.

It was rare for Fingers even to attend a Summer People cocktail party. He avoided them like daytime TV. But this one was different. It had been given by a couple whose brief and casual acquaintance had been a pleasure to him. Three years ago they had moved to Oregon. No sooner were they settled than the husband was thrown twenty-five feet by a car that struck the bicycle he was riding. He was in a coma for three months. Doctors told his wife he would surely die. He sustained a smashed hip and enough other breaks and contusions to render him useless. He was a geologist and avid skin diver. He was a soccer player and sailor. Now he was barely alive. To make matters worse, right after he came out of the coma an over-enthusiastic doctor who had misread the X rays had him hauled out of bed and taken on forced "therapeutic" walks on his smashed hip.

Under normal circumstances Fingers would have shrunk from cocktail party attention of any sort. The presence of his hosts made the attention even harder to bear. The enormity of their ordeal—the constant pain of the physical rehabilitation battle that had brought the husband onto crutches after two and a half years; the incessant demand that the wife focus attention exclusively on his and their two children's needs; and the untold hospital horrors—had been clearly set in their faces. The list of specialists that had been consulted—the psychiatrists and psychologists and all the social workers and volunteers—filled a large address book. And the two of them were still hanging in there, shadows of their former vivacious selves, still able to summon the energy to keep their act together. Theirs was surely the stuff of real heroism.

Talking with this couple made Fingers realize that he had in fact not been scared at sea. It was a question he had to reexamine, given the skepticism with which his denial had been received. He wondered about it himself. Why hadn't he been scared? He had been apprehensive a few times (viewing the future with anxiety), but not scared: He experienced no widespread state of alarm. Then what did scare him?

Unbridled anger scared him, his and that of others. He remembered an evening at prep school when the football captain and one of the more portly down linemen decided to beat on him and his roommate just to pass the time. He had been scared then. Not because he happened to be the carbon copy of the skinny kid in the ads who got sand kicked in his face at the beach. Not because the beating was severe. It wasn't. It was more like harassment punctuated with arm and leg noogies. Painful harassment, and in the supposed privacy of his own room. As the fun progressed, a red film lowered across Fingers's eyes, and then all he could think about was the belt knife in the top drawer of his desk, the knife that he kept sharp as a razor, that could come to life in his hand before anybody knew it. The football captain and his down lineman got bored and left before it happened, but it had been close. It took Fingers days to recover from that trip to the edge.

Physical pain scared him too. As a kid he had grown up on Saturday matinees of war movies. For years he had been obsessed by what a bullet would feel like entering his back, thudding into his chest, shattering his knee. The scene that always got him was the aerial dogfight sequence, with engines wailing and wing cannons spitting fire and death. There would always be close-ups of pilots in their cockpits. The hole would appear in the Perspex canopy a millisecond before the pilot would be slammed against the headrest, his eyes rolling as the blood poured across his face from beneath his helmet. It was a scene that numbed Fingers's testicles. He spent many hours silently pleading for the war to end before he was old enough to participate. He knew he would never be brave enough for it.

In Greece a few years ago, he had met a tour guide who had been imprisoned after the military coup. Her tales of torture, of the beatings with sticks on the bottoms of the feet, of people lowered into water in burlap bags tied at their necks in which several cats had been placed, brought on the old war-movie reaction. And after seeing the film Midnight Express, a graphic tale of torture and madness in a Turkish prison, he had had two weeks of dreams that drenched him in cold sweat.

As he talked with his friends at the cocktail party, as the story of their crisis unfolded, as the smallest details colored their experience with terrible poignancy, he knew their plight frightened him very much. Physical disability. How he might contend with being paralyzed, or blinded, or deformed puzzled him greatly. He suspected he would not be brave enough for it.

At 5:30 a.m., with the gray dawn still a dream on the horizon, *Kialoa* rounded Bishop Rock, turned the corner. Sheets were eased as the boat headed for England with the wind at her back. Fingers never saw the Bishop. The crew had been going below in pairs all night to grab an hour's respite and to change to dry clothing if they chose. He went below at 5 a.m. At six, when he was roused from the hollow sleep of exhaustion, the boat was no longer heaving and slamming, pitching and rolling.

Kialoa passed Bishop Rock four or more miles to port, which sounded good as a safety margin, but plainly it was too wide for racing. Back at Fastnet Rock, *Kialoa* had been barely making the course to the Bishop by steering hard on the wind. After forty miles or so, the wind came aft until it was on the beam during the storm. But the waves were driving the boat to leeward. After the runner broke and structural damage to the mast was suspected, it was even more important to hold high of the course. It would not do to miss the Bishop, and have to go hard on the wind to round it. Nor would it be prudent to pass too close to the deadly, rock-strewn Scilly Islands, possibly to enrich their long and gruesome history of marine disaster with yet another hapless vessel, another toll of dead. Going to weather in such a blow and sea condition would have been a tall order even for *Kialoa*. Much as he might deny it, every man who drove *Kialoa* that night had been cheating toward the right side of the course. Other boats were similarly hedging their bets. One of the U.S. Admiral's Cup boats passed the Bishop twenty miles to port, an outrageous error. *Kialoa*'s four-mile error would cost enough.

Fingers got his first look at the storm he had been in for the past seven hours. The sun rose brilliantly in a clear sky, highlighting the white foaming caps of huge breaking seas on all sides. The ocean was in an awful frenzy. The local waves were less confused. Perhaps influenced by the shoal that runs from Land's End, England, out to the Scillies, they were lining up with some regularity from the west. Now they had a rhythm, and they were even larger than before. Streaks of wind raced down their fronts into the troughs and up the backs of the next like schools of small fish in full panic. *Kialoa* chased after them, pursued in turn by thirty-five-foot walls of deep blue water that hung heavily—but now without menace—above the stern. *Kialoa* began surfing like a dinghy. Sheets of glistening water flew from her bow as if from a water ski in a tight turn. Her speed never dropped below fifteen knots. Planing on one set of waves that must have measured forty feet, the speed gauge registered an incredible twenty-one knots.

Planing on a sailboat is one of the great thrills. Planing is a state wherein the hull skims over the water rather than driving through it. Certain conditions are required for it to happen. There must be plenty of wind. A steady pattern of good-sized waves helps. The shape of the hull is critical. Sailing dinghies that plane have been around for a long time. Typically they are round-bottomed boats that present a wide, flattish surface to the water. Their profile tapers from bow to stern with the flowing curve of a hunting knife's cutting edge. When they are steered off the wind in planing conditions, their centerboards are retracted until only a little fin remains underwater for stability. They begin to lift, and off they go like wild things, dashing and careening across the water—trying to fly—their breathless crews struggling to maintain control. They are high-performance, unforgiving little packets of dynamite. Just thinking about what they can do can make a sailor alternately smile and tremble in his sleep.

Sailing a boat on a full-out plane is the essence of sensuality. The harder the wind blows and the steeper the seas, the faster the boat goes in its mad, futile attempt to become airborne, the closer it brings the crew to the edge of delirium, an edge that is unmistakably orgasmic. Planing, for Fingers, had always provided insatiable ecstasy. Years ago, when he had first become proficient with one-man planing boats, he would wait for heavy weather. Then he would launch, and tear back and forth across the bay for hours at a time. His fatigue would be suppressed by the satisfaction of the boat's responsiveness, of the way it surged and vibrated beneath him. Across the bay he would go, one more time, one more time. He wouldn't realize until he finally came in that his hands had been rubbed raw by the mainsheet, that his legs were cramped, his knees wobbly.

A friend of his who worked for a time at various Club Meds in the course of his devoted study of getting women into bed had assured him that certain sailboats, like muscle cars, were extensions of the male phallus. He spoke particularly of the catamaran, which virtually planes standing still. You just picked out some girl on the beach, his friend told him, and asked her to go sailing. Then you got going, lifted a hull, the spray flew, and now you had this girl in an active, wet situation. You were in control. The rest was easy. Fingers could believe it. His friend's research had been thorough.

Only in recent years had planing capability come to the larger boats. Larger boats were always in the heavy-displacement category. Their hulls were deep forward and aft, with keels that tapered gradually into the rise of the topsides. Their shapes condemned them to always go through the water. Their "hull speeds"—absolute limits at which they could move through the water—were calculable. Lately, however, light-displacement boats have been built in all sizes. It has taken time, and the light-displacement concept has proven not only faster but, in the hands of experts, almost as seaworthy. Large racing hulls are now designed after the small, high-performance boats. The keels are large thin fins that are bolted on after the hull is finished. Turn these boats off the wind, set a spinnaker, and speeds of fifteen knots are common. The best a heavy displacement boat of comparable size could do was nine.

Planing on a boat *Kialoa*'s size is a memorable thrill ride. Suddenly a yacht of seventy-nine feet feels like a boat one-fourth her size. The stately queen of the fleet begins behaving like Lolita.

With her bow hanging out of a wave as she took the drop, *Kialoa* felt light as a feather and in full control. The crew sat on the deck in stoned silence, marveling at her performance. With tense concentration, the helmsman would spin the big chrome wheel with quick hands, settling her in the groove as her stern rose on a wave, then break into a grin as she took off on her own, roaring and trembling, as the speed gauge rose toward twenty. Spontaneous cheers erupted from us as we urged her on. For seven hours, until we neared the finish line at Plymouth, we sailed like that.

Ocean races are sustained by goals. Winning underlies the effort, but less comprehensive, more immediate goals are what keep the boat moving, the crew alert. Goals are formulated, then checked off or abandoned as new ones take their place. *Kialoa* got a good start. Check. She was first to Fastnet Rock. Check. Then the course record came up. Unless the storm were followed by a dead calm, that was a virtual check. Then someone mentioned the possibility of finishing in under three days, and slowly that absurd notion caught fire. That would mean cutting more than seven hours off *American Eagle*'s record, but as we planed toward England amidst the flying spray, it looked more and more like a serious possibility.

For several hours after rounding the Bishop, *Kialoa* sailed with the main still triple-reefed, and a small jib set out to windward on the spinnaker pole. Setting a spinnaker was only lightly considered. With the boat running before the wind at an average of twelve to fifteen knots, the true wind speed over the deck was reduced to around fifty knots. Tangling with *Kialoa*'s smallest and heaviest spinnaker in that much wind—and given the steep, formidable seas— would be a nightmare. Maybe the boat would be controllable. But in such conditions a broach would be inevitable. A broach is one of the more frightening maneuvers a yacht can perform. It begins with a lapse of concentration by the helmsman, or a lump of sea that lifts the stern at the wrong time, interfering with steerage, or a sudden gust of wind that drives the boat to windward. Or all of the above. As the boat veers and brings the wind more on the beam, the spinnaker rotates to leeward, still full, dragging the boat down on its side. Then there is not much to do but hang on and wait for the spinnaker to collapse, the puff to ease up, or for something to break. Sometimes it is possible to release the spinnaker sheet—if someone can lower himself down a deck that has become a nearly vertical wall. A broach is a horror in smooth water. In big seas, it is worse than that.

There was also the mast to consider. The true state of its health was still in question. It was important to remember the priorities. *Kialoa* was racing to finish. And to break the course record. In that order. So Bruce Kendall said no chute. Fingers was sitting on the deck getting itchy and wondering why. It dawned on him that he was thinking about the spinnaker. Thinking it should be set. The boat was a touch underpowered. She was losing a lot of speed between waves. Bruce had admitted that. But Fingers didn't speak his piece. He kept his mouth shut. He wouldn't be the guy who pulled the string on the monster. He wouldn't be responsible for having three tigers by their tails. How easy it was to second-guess. If that responsibility had been his, he surely would have kept the thing in the bag. But he bet it would have been quite a ride to have it up. He chastised himself as a thrill seeker and tried to think about something else.

[Kendall was right about the mast. Postrace examination revealed two substantial cracks near the staysail sheave box that had obviously been sustained when the runner block parted. Why the stick remained standing for the duration of the race is still a mystery to all concerned.]

When *Kialoa* passed Lizard Point abeam—a light on the southwest tip of Great Britain—three-day fever was rampant among the crew. There were forty-five miles to the finish from that point, and we had just over four hours to make it. It was going to be close.

Several of the crew picked up the time on their watches, and the countdown began. The wind dropped five knots or so when we entered the English Channel, but we still had plenty of speed. Gradually we increased power by shaking out the reef in the mainsail.

With about an hour to go, Jim Kilroy appeared on deck. Without help from anyone, he had managed to haul himself and his two broken ribs out of his bunk, shave, take a shower, powder his feet (undoubtedly), and put on clean clothes. It was remarkable. People stared at him in amazement. "I've never finished a race on my back," Jim said by way of explanation.

Forty-five minutes from the finish line we jibed and set *Kialoa*'s biggest reaching jib. The seas were much smoother in the Channel, and the boat powered toward the line at a steady twelve knots. The countdown continued. We had fifteen minutes to make it. We had ten. Through binoculars we could see race committee people atop the tall light tower that marks the entrance to Plymouth harbor.

Plymouth harbor. To the left was the little island behind which Sir Francis Drake anchored the Golden Hind in 1580 when he returned from sacking Spanish ships of a fortune in gold and jewels. Drake's Island, it has been called ever since. Plymouth, where the Mayflower put in for repairs; her point of departure for the New World. Plymouth, strategic guardian of the western entrance to the English Channel, a large harbor with a deep-water approach, the greatest naval arsenal in the world in the late nineteenth century. In the awful blitz of 1941, the Germans destroyed all of Plymouth's principal streets and buildings. But they could not destroy the lovely green hills that rise sharply from the shoreline, or the rugged charm that comes from ages of cohabitation with the sea and those who sail upon it.

With five minutes to go we neared the line. With four minutes we knew we had it made. Under three days! As the watches ran down to three minutes we crossed the line: bam! The gun! It was a joyous moment. Our fatigue miraculously lifted. Jim's smile was wide (he was careful not to laugh). The hand shaking and back slapping all around were plentiful. We doused sails and cleaned up the deck in high spirits. Beer was broken out. The engine was started. Then we motored around the high stone wall that hides the docks of Plymouth and saw *Condor* made fast to the pier.

Condor must have been a mirage. Perhaps it had broken down and had come in early. Maybe the yacht missed the Bishop and just sailed on in. *Condor* simply could not have beaten us. But the sad truth of it was plain even before we swung in a circle to lay alongside, even before we recognized the cluttered look of a yacht that had only recently finished an ocean race (preceding us by thirty minutes), even before we gazed into the haggard faces of the crew, a group that had the drained, spaced-out look of people who had put several lost weekends back to back, who had been face to face with demons; a deathly, wasted look tempered by the sweet glow of accomplishment. *Condor* wouldn't win. Under the handicapping system, it had to give up too much time to smaller boats.

But this powerful boat had gotten the big gun, the first gun, and she had set a Fastnet record that would last a very long time.

The *Condor* crew studied the disappointment and disbelief on our faces as we sought to comprehend their triumph. It was like a scene on the gridiron after a tough game that has been decided by one point. Both boats had survived and done a good job of it. Both crews were relieved to be in. A lot of mutual admiration was exchanged in the cold beers that were handed across the lifelines.

Condor wasn't the only reception committee, even though the finish of an ocean race is too unpredictable to attract a crowd. The lead boats most often finish solely under the eyes of the race committee. When they land at the dock they are lucky if some spare soul is around to take their lines. But at Plymouth, above our heads on the pier, a small group of people had collected. Some of the faces were recognizable as wives of sailors on other boats. Most of them had friends or relatives still bobbing on the Irish Sea, or so they fervently hoped. They were not waiting to congratulate us. It was a silent crowd. The faces were grim. A few shed anxious tears.

Theirs would be a long wait. The next boat to finish would be six hours behind *Kialoa*.

Jim Kilroy was helped over the lifelines onto *Condor*, where he congratulated owner Bob Bell. Bell stood his ground, waiting for Kilroy to come to him. His look of pride was unmistakable. "Got you" it said. It was the first time in fourteen meetings that

Condor had beaten *Kialoa* boat for boat, and Bell was enjoying. Somehow Kilroy negotiated the vertical metal ladder that rose fifteen feet to the pier, and made it upright to the waiting ambulance, to go off for X- rays and treatment.

From comparing notes after the race, it appeared that *Condor* and *Kialoa* had rounded the Bishop at about the same time. *Condor* had made up the hour it had lost on the first leg during the one-hundred-fifty-mile leg from Fastnet Rock during the storm. *Condor* is a more rugged boat than *Kialoa*. It was built for the round-the-world race. It is stiffer. Its rigging is a size larger. It had no breakdowns on the way to the Bishop. Having rounded Fastnet an hour after *Kialoa*, *Condor* was enabled by the rapidly veering wind to steer more directly toward the Bishop, sail more on the rhumb line. *Condor* also gained materially during the hour that *Kialoa* was proceeding at half speed. And most significantly, the afterguard decided to cut Bishop Rock close. They decided to aim right at it and hope they called it correctly. If they misjudged it, they figured they would simply bear away, leaving the Scilly Islands on the wrong side, and drop out of the race. It would be all or nothing, because the extreme course change it would take to miss the Scilly Islands would have to be made at the last minute, and the avoidance of disaster would take superb navigation combined with more luck than might have been available that morning.

They called it right, and cut it close. They took a sizable risk, hung the boat and its crew of twenty right out over the edge. They passed Bishop Rock half a mile to port. Even in the darkness they were close enough to see the great seas smashing themselves against the rocks with spectacular explosions that ricocheted tons of white foam skyward like phosphorus from detonating artillery shells. They had stuck one foot into the mouth of the abyss and pulled it out again.

Kialoa was far enough outside to prevent the two boats from seeing one another in the gray first light. So the first thought *Condor*'s crew had after putting the jaws of the Bishop safely behind them was the same thought they had been having all night: where is *Kialoa*? But no one spoke about it. Their relief at finding the Bishop and rounding it properly, and without incident, lasted them a full hour. Then they discussed the situation. They asked themselves if they could have lost anything? They didn't think so. Could they have driven the boat harder? No. They had really given it the whip. Now was no time to ease up. There were a hundred miles to the finish. And they might still be playing catch-up.

As the sun rose in front of them, aboard *Condor* they struggled to shake one reef out of the main. Then they hauled out a large foresail called a "blast reacher" because of the immense pulling power it affords on a reach, and set it to windward on the spinnaker pole. A small, reefed spinnaker staysail—a light sail designed to work as a partner with the spinnaker -- added one and a quarter knots to their speed. Now they were flying.

It wasn't until 11 a.m. that Geoff Prior suggested the spinnaker. Prior is a Kiwi who was working for Hood Sails. He and skipper Peter Blake were running the boat for owner Bob Bell of Bermuda. Bell is a newcomer to the sport who is content to pay the bills, watch, and learn.

"We've got to be crazy. That is what we said when we decided to set that chute," Prior recalled.

"We talked about it a very long time. We spent a lot of time analyzing what might have happened during the night. If we were ahead, we had to defend our position. If we were behind, we had to attack. We knew we were crazy even to be out there. If we set the chute we would really be nuts. The crew was ready. They would have taken anything. I don't think any of them realized what could have happened."

Prior and Blake decided to set *Condor*'s heaviest, stretchiest big yellow spinnaker. They stopped it at intervals with black plastic strips torn from garbage bags. They hoisted it to the masthead like a great yellow, black-striped snake. They waited until the boat settled in the groove of a wave, and then broke it out. Kaaawump! The boat leaned forward under the sudden strain like a running back hitting the line of scrimmage. The speed jumped instantly from sixteen to twenty knots. "We went off in this one wave," Prior said, "and the boat thundered. The speed gauge hit twenty-nine knots." Twenty-nine knots on a seventy-seven-foot sailboat!

With wind and seas astern, the sun was the ruling element that morning. Crewmen gratefully shed safety harnesses, foul-weather gear, boots, and several wet layers in hopes of savoring its warmth. *Condor's* crew was in just such a relaxed state when the boat broached for the first time. It was a most spectacular broach. *Condor* spun out like a race car hitting oil, driving its shoulder down and rounding up into the wind, or trying to with the chute dragging the mast down parallel to the sea. The crew grabbed what they could and hung on as the deck became the bulkhead. When *Condor* finally spilled its chute and came up, it was head to wind. The spinnaker backed against the mast and rigging and began driving the boat backwards at five knots. Somehow it spun again, and again took off in the proper direction, spinnaker full once again, speed climbing above twenty-five.

"Everybody was stunned," Prior said. "Too stunned to speak. Finally one of the guys working the bow asked if he might have permission to go below so he could change his underpants. That broke the spell."

The crew scrambled back into their gear and harnesses. It was well they did. There were two more broaches like the first. Then *Condor* pearled. "Pearling," a term borrowed from oyster diving, is a rare occurrence. It can happen downwind in extreme wind and sea conditions when a high-performance boat is overpowered with sail. Surfing down one wave, the boat drives into the next. Its speed overcomes the marginal buoyancy characteristic of its bow, and it plunges in and begins to dive. The weight of water accumulating on the deck assures its descent. The only way for it to get out is to stop and lever out as it falls on its side. That is what *Condor* did. It buried its bow to the base of the mast before the dive stopped.

"Our hatches were shut," Prior said, "but the ventilators took in water. We had a foot of water over the floorboards after it was over. We were up to our waists in water in the cockpit. We just drove it under. If we were crazy to be out there, and nuts to have the chute up, now we were being idiots."

Condor had carried its chute for two hours. Now they took it down. "Putting it up was the wrong move," Prior said in retrospect. "We could have torn out the rig. We could have killed people." As it was, they ripped out a huge turning block on the stern for the spinnaker guy, and lost three stanchions in the process. A crewman in the wrong place was whipped badly in the legs by the runaway guy. The stern pulpit was torn off, and they lost both radio aerials.

They regrouped. They put the blast reacher back on the spinnaker pole. Five minutes later they saw *Kialoa* for the first time, as a tiny triangle of white—astern.

Sitting in a bar in Newport, Rhode Island, one rainy night not long after the Fastnet Race was over, Fingers asked Prior why they had done it. What had been the deciding factor in his and Peter Blake's deliberations? What prompted them to set the spinnaker in such incredible conditions?

Prior stared at his drink for a moment. Then he looked up.

"We were racing," Prior said.

Parting was neither sweet nor sorrowful. Cowes Week was over. Our leader had been unceremoniously trucked off to the hospital. There were airplanes to make. Schedules of life that had been suspended rushed back with urgency. There was a certain amount of exhilaration (accomplishment) shared by the crew for having made it through this storm, but it was unspoken. This was a very seasoned bunch. Cool hands. The implication was that they had seen worse, or at least as bad. And if one kept sailing, there would surely be another and another. Best not get too steamed up. Tread softly.

So we broke out some rum while we crammed our duffel bags with wet gear and made small talk. Then we shook hands all around and scattered to the winds. It was just like the old days, when a whaling crew broke up after a two-year voyage. Joseph Conrad would have been proud.

Having been flung ashore at Plymouth, Fingers sought lodging. He had shunned the Holiday Inn in favor of experiencing some local color, "bed and breakfast," as the little signs advertised. The only problem was that most of the little signs were covered over by another little sign that read "full." He must have walked for more than an hour, working his way along the quaint little streets that lead away from the waterfront, his sea bag full of wet garments threatening to wear through hands already chafed from working the boat for three days. Having had one hour's rest in twenty-four, having enjoyed several rum and Cokes on board to fortify him for his venture ashore, he was beyond fatigue, floating in some kind of strange travelogue where people drove cars on the wrong side of streets and spoke in question marks.

When weariness prevailed he stopped at a pay phone, put two pence in the slot, and tried to tell the cab dispatcher where he was. He sat on the curb with his gear like an evicted tenant and dozed. In only forty-five minutes the cab pulled up. It was driven by an affable man named Paddy (what else?) and of course Paddy had a friend who might have a room. Three stops later Fingers found a vacancy. It was a small room, he was told. As long as it was large enough to fit a bed, he responded. The lady smiled. The room reminded him of the old Henny Youngman routine about being so small that when you put the key in the door you broke the window on the opposite wall. It was that small. It was also candy pink. Candy-pink walls. Candy-pink curtains. Candy-pink bedspread. There was one foot of space on each side of the saggy bed. It didn't matter. It was a bed. Now for a shower, a long-awaited shower.

He went down the hall to the bathroom. It was in use. He waited. Still in use. Finally he got in. There was no shower. He drew a tub, kneeled in the lukewarm water, and tried to wash his hair. As the blood rushed to his head and the soap ran into his eyes, total comprehension came to him for the first time about how the Pilgrims—his forefathers—could have preferred an ocean crossing of inestimable length and hardship on a vessel of marginal sea-worthiness bound for a land of unknown hostility and danger, to life in England. He made friends with the rooming-house cat and counted one hundred rings for the overseas operator before he gave up and slept like a rock in his candy-pink bed.

In the morning he sought out the landlord to settle up. The daily tabloid had just arrived with its grim headlines of death and destruction, its photographs of ruined vessels and air-sea rescue efforts. It was the first Fingers knew of the extent of the storm's damage to the fleet. The landlord noticed his interest in the newspaper, and asked if he had been in the race. "You mean," the man said, "we very nearly didn't get your business?"

Fingers went to the docks in mid-morning as a spectator to see what boats had come in and find out how the others were faring. It was a beautiful morning, sunny and warm with blue skies and a light breeze. As he crossed the Hoe, a limestone bastion a hundred-twenty feet above the sea whose flat expanse was large enough to accommodate almost all of Plymouth's quarter-million inhabitants, Fingers could see a well-spaced procession of yachts running toward the finish line under spinnaker. The long line of flags that lent flourish to the hilltop where it is said Drake was bowling when he received the news that the Spanish Armada had been sighted, were waving lazily. Britons on holiday strolled in family units, and bought sweets and ice cream from carts parked along the road next to the seawall. The scene was travel-poster idyllic.

It was difficult to imagine the ferocity of the

storm that had lashed this historic oceanfront just the previous day.

The Royal Ocean Racing Club (RORC), sponsors of the Fastnet Race, had set up shop in a small dock-side building. Three women volunteers were manning the phones and posting notices. Under normal circumstances the setup would have sufficed. Given the proportions of the marine disaster which had occurred, and which had been amplified worldwide as only concentrated media coverage can do it, the office had long since ceased to function in any meaningful way. Doubtless with good intentions the RORC telephone number had been flashed on the television news coverage of the event. The result was that many Britons with only third- or fourth-hand acquaintance of a crewman were ringing in. And since fifty-seven Admiral's Cup boats representing nineteen countries had been in the race, overseas lines were jammed as well. The three lines into the office were hopelessly tangled. Calls out were impossible. The crowd of anxious people wedged in front of the impromptu counter was trying hard to be understanding and patient. The volunteer women were trying to be sympathetic and patient themselves. Occasionally someone would post a new notice on the bulletin board outside. But its content would be hours old, hardly sufficient to slake the urgency of those for whom waiting was an agony.

Fifty to a hundred people had gathered outside the RORC office. They were friends and relatives of sailors yet to be accounted for, accompanied by sailors they knew who had finished. They talked quietly, the sailors sharing storm stories calculated to bring laughter, ease tension. Or telling of a radio contact here, passing a rumor there establishing that a certain boat was probably still racing, or still sailing, or at least still floating. And from in front of the RORC office one had a clear view of the end of the huge seawall and the yachts coming around it into the harbor as they finished, at the rate of about ten an hour. Every boat that finished brought new hope for those as yet unreported. Only eighty-five boats would finish. One hundred ninety-four boats retired to nearby ports. Twenty-four boats were abandoned, of which nineteen were recovered.

On one edge of this anxious crowd a familiar figure had claimed a sizable pacing and strutting area for himself. With the freshly laundered white pants, the white sweater with the name of his twelve-meter embroidered upon it (*Courageous*), the mustache, the mirrored sunglasses, the navy blue yachting cap, and the big cigar, it could have been none other than Atlanta's independent television and professional sports magnate, Ted Turner. If there was any doubt, the high volume and cliched content of his remarks would have erased it. He was known as "the mouth of the South" with reason. This morning, in the midst of a lot of people who were visibly strung out behind the possibility of very bad news, Turner was broadcasting his own anxiety fit. His blinding concern, it appeared, was that one of the smaller boats with a large handicap allowance might finish in time to take the overall victory from *Tenacious*, Turner's yacht. Turner paced to and fro as he waved his cigar and talked a blue streak, giving one the strange impression that the movements of his feet were generating the sounds from his mouth.

Several of his crew were in attendance, supporting him like rigging supports a mast. After each of his profane inquiries about whether or not a specific boat had finished, and how much time *Tenacious* had to give the SOB, one of his crew would run to the bulletin board to check once again. After each of his expansive attempts at humor, others of his crew would provide the canned laughter. If his cigar needed relighting, a match would appear. Fingers had heard from several students of the sport that Turner won yacht races regularly not just because of the great amounts of time, energy, and money he invested, but because no one else wanted to win as badly as he did. Indeed, Fingers had never seen the desire to win taken to such an indecent level.

Turner was apparently still overcome by the frenzy of winning when he told the press, "There's no use crying over the dead. The King is dead; long live the King. That ain't the ultimate storm... ." Later, in an "exclusive," bylined piece in *Motor Boating* and *Sailing* (October 1979), Turner recalled the night of the storm in his best down-home, shucks-it-was-nothin' tone: "Throughout the night we just hung on and I steered. . . It was all I could do to steer and watch the sail. I had one of the crew stand next to the binnacle and read off the compass headings as the boat lurched down the course. When a big sea would well up behind us, I bore off and rode it down."

What puzzled Fingers was that some people who had crewed aboard *Tenacious* told him that Turner had been below decks for all but two-and-a-half hours of the storm. Turner was a first-rate racing sailor, a master of race-boat organization, a good helmsman whose record in all kinds of boats over the years would be difficult to match. But he shared with other racing helmsmen, an aversion to heavy weather. Fingers was reminded of an old children's song about a ship called The Walloping Window Blind, in which went in part:

The man at the wheel was said to feel
contempt for the wildest blow
but it often appeared when the gale had cleared
that he'd been in his bunk below.

Fingers could even remember the tune.

At Boston's Logan Airport Fingers' woman was crying. His arrival wasn't a surprise. He had finally been able to summon the patience needed to locate the overseas operator. So his woman knew he was alive and kicking. But she, like the rest of the sailors' stateside kin, had been whipped up by erroneous and overblown press reports. The hysteria mongers of the Fourth Estate had been at it again with the lies by omission, the panic by suggestion, the talk of boats falling off the sides of waves. Their technique of picking out the most newsworthy name and turning "has yet to be heard from" into "reported missing" in the interest of sustaining viewer-ship (readership) was reprehensible. And so former British Prime Minister Edward Heath, a long-time ocean-racing enthusiast, was reported missing. And Ted Turner was reported missing. But Turner, the eventual Fastnet winner, was definitely not missing. Neither was Heath.

Nonetheless, it moved Fingers to see his woman crying. It was like a sneak preview of one's funeral. It was nice to be missed, even when a solo gig was on the docket as an imminent event, as a possible antidote to the fifteen-year hitch. Her crying said something nice about those fifteen years.

Solo. Without companion. Alone. Fingers and his woman had been using that word rather than the more common, legal-sounding term. "Solo" had had Outward Bound origins. Fingers had taken an Outward Bound course at the Hurricane Island School in Maine and had loved it. There, "solo" consisted of three days on a tiny island, alone, with minimal rations. It was a part of the course that made students particularly apprehensive. In recent years the rations had been increased to put the emphasis less on physical survival and more on confrontation with self. That made students even more apprehensive. With good reason. One has to spend too much time with oneself as it is.

Fingers was an only child who knew how to spend time alone. Sometimes he even relished it. But he was apprehensive about this solo. Maybe he feared he needed it too much. He knew why it was called for. It had to do partly with all those weird fragments of people, conversations, and cultural extracts that he had been harboring for years. Too much strange baggage on his side of the scale. Even among the overwhelming number of good moments, there were too many bad moments that were indelible. None was very big. It was always a buildup of fragments. Then something would come along like the Himalayan storm and all those fragments would be melted (and expanded) into one great lump of contention by the fierce heat generated. And the lump would end up in the middle of an often-trod path and become an obstruction. Only dynamite could budge it, and even in the most experienced hands that was going to make bad smoke, bad noise, and stop the birds singing for an indeterminate amount of time.

What depressed Fingers was the awful inevitability of such an impasse, especially in the best of times. Wars, recessions, famines, droughts, hostile Indians, and the like always seemed to have a unifying effect on people, on couples, and on relationships. The frontier theory. Man did like to be known by his adversity, by the nature of how he had responded to his share of abuse. But in "the best of times" something went awry. Perhaps it was because people were so unused to that condition. In any case, expectations soared. Overreaching ran rampant. The whole country began living the Rubaiyat of Omar Khayyam, began eating, drinking, and being merry with a vengeance against the possibility that tomorrow might bring hard rain, or the China Syndrome.

Certainly one could argue that it was hardly the best of times. But there was no war, no blood-thirsty Indians, no depression, and recession was still in the staging area. Whereas one could hate Nixon, one could only feel sorry for Jimmy Carter. There was an energy crisis on paper, and an assortment of average life-sized problems, but nothing all-encompassing. If it wasn't the best of times, what was?

The fair-share concept had spun about-face as people used their little plastic cards—their "clout" —to prove they could get satisfaction, buy it at the store, in fact. As a result, dissatisfaction was having a field day. Because the new cars had to be a disappointment, and even if the reception was good there was damn little to save for posterity on the new video recorder. The swimming pool got green and scummy unless you spent half the damn time cleaning it, and the collective output of riding lawn mowers and high-powered stereo systems and snow blowers and electric-grid bug fryers and neighborhood disco parlors and CB sets often triggered the smoke alarm system, for some strange reason.

Puzzled, and with time on their hands thanks to microwave ovens and all the rest, people looked at each other and began to wonder. Suddenly the psychiatrists and jogging stores were doing big business as people began picking and digging at their various relationships, in many cases disturbing perfectly good caulking in their obsessive efforts to eliminate the tiniest and most infrequent drips. And a new song was atop the charts. It had changed from "I can't get no . . ." to "I can't get enough!" Too delicate for the world? Certainly a possibility.

Fingers's solo began with a week in Cambridge, Massachusetts. He was idly browsing in a Harvard Square bookshop thinking about such things when the captivating sound of his favorite broadcast personality—National Public Radio's Susan Stamberg on the program "All Things Considered"—came through to him from a speaker buried in the books three bays down. He rushed toward the voice that could soothe savage breasts and browsed under the speaker while she interviewed P. J. O'Rourke, editor-in-chief of the National Lampoon, on the demise of the MG. Fingers had heard the news with sadness the previous day that British Leyland was discontinuing what was once the most popular sports car in the United States. Fingers had owned one. A 1952 TD. A classic.

"You could lie back and put your silly tweed cap on and coast through the countryside almost without effort," O'Rourke was saying. "Of course they are a miserable automobile, broken all the time, no heat, the top won't go up, won't go down, the windows fall off—but if you think about the kind of guy who had an MG you can see why they are gone. The whole reason to have an MG was to get girls, and girls no longer go for the type of loon who runs around in an open sports car that probably isn't insured right, with no seatbelt on, no crash helmet, no roll bar. His insurance rates are going to be high, and he doesn't care about the whales, and is probably perfectly willing to eat foods with additives in them and who knows what else."

Even in a bookshop in dour old Harvard Square people were chuckling, even in Harvard Square where burnt-out Ph.D. candidates were occasionally seen babbling profanity in the streets. Even a few women browsers in search of salvation through literature had turned toward the speaker and were smiling bittersweet smiles at the way we were.

Susan Stamberg asked O'Rourke what we were losing with the demise of such a car.

"Fun!" O'Rourke said. "Fun has gone out of style. The MG was part of the devil-may-care days, no belts, no roll bar, they weren't a bit safe, and the idea was to drive them fast as heck and take chances and live life to the fullest. Not a particularly popular philosophy at the moment."

A month later, still on solo, Fingers found himself at a friend's farm in Maryland, in the Police State of Maryland, where the roads were literally infested with the yellow-peril cars of the state troopers, cars bristling with radar and driven by a paramilitary force of TV-styled cops with drill-sergeant dispositions who firmly believed that people who drove faster than fifty-five miles per hour were not only Communists but potential ax murderers.

Maryland was a place whose water-moccasin police had been known to issue a fifty-dollar ticket to people for sailing their Sunfish without life jackets on board. But Maryland was it for the moment. Fingers had been out of commission for nearly three weeks after the extraction of a large tooth that had left an infected dry socket in its wake. The steady diet of pain-killers had combined with the debilitating effect of the infection to make full-time sleeping the only sensible course. As a result, he was bed-weary and cranky. So the very first moment he had felt the slightest bit better, he began eyeing his friend's eighteen-foot catamaran, moored in the estuary adjacent to the farm, thinking that if he didn't get off his ass soon and do something, he would develop a serious case of the don't-give-a-damns.

It happened that the moment he felt the slightest bit better was at 5 p.m. on a chilly, gray October day that promised rain. No matter. He pulled on his wet suit, rigged the cat, and sailed out toward the river on a freshening breeze.

A half hour later the breeze had increased to a steady fifteen knots, and a light, misty rain was falling. It would be dark early, so Fingers turned the cat and started in. Now it was fast. One hull lifted, and then a series of puffs came out of nowhere, as puffs do in the Chesapeake area. The hull lifted precariously. The last yellow pain-killer hadn't quite worn off, and Fingers's reactions were slow. And he had found the main sheet on this little-used boat submerged and covered with barnacles. He had worked on it, but it was still stiff. He let it go too late, and then it didn't run out as quickly as it should. Over he went. Son of a bitch. God damn. There was something marvelously ludicrous and properly humiliating about sitting like a bump on the high hull of an overturned catmaran in the gray rain, in a freshening breeze, in the gathering dusk. He was glad he had the wet suit on. This could be a long night.

Raising an overturned small sailboat is not a problem. One stands on the centerboard, hops off as the boat comes up, and then clambers in and begins bailing and sailing at the same time.

A catamaran is another story. Especially an eighteen-footer with only one person on board. The wide Dacron trampoline stretched between the hulls that functions as a deck acts as a sail when the boat is on its side. No leverage is possible. Fingers knew that to raise the boat he would have to get it ashore. The closest shore, as he was being blown, was about five miles downriver. He was drifting along at maybe one knot. Five hours. Unless he could persuade the boat closer to the point of nearby land he would pass on the left. He removed a centerboard. Sitting on the lower hull, he used it as a paddle.

The scheme worked. In a half hour he was in close enough to walk. He pulled the sails off, raised the twin rudders, removed the other centerboard, and dragged the boat in as close to the rocky shore as possible. There was one spot where it just fit between rocks. Holding the mast at fingertip height above his head, on tiptoe, wasn't quite enough to get it past its balance point. So he made a pile of rocks and rubble. When he stood on the pile it might be enough. The first two tries he fell, nearly crowning himself with the heavy mast. The third try he made it. The boat hesitated (the wind was still against the trampoline), then dropped down on both its hulls. An hour had elapsed since he went over.

Fingers re-rigged the boat, raised the sails and shoved off into the river. He checked for damage. The boat hadn't been so much as scuffed. One of his flip-flops was gone, and the foot it belonged to was bleeding from the heel. But what the hell, he was back up, heading for the barn. And he hadn't even gotten arrested.

He took off for the farm on the freshening breeze, strapping the sheet down, easing one hull up, going like hell, spray flying, the boat groaning sensually as catamarans do at speed, and he laughed aloud into the gray, rainy dusk. It wasn't a laugh of arrogance (tread softly!) or even satisfaction. He was just feeling good. His dry socket had stopped hurting. He was in his element. He was alive.

Made in the USA
San Bernardino, CA
22 July 2019